A Seat at The Table

Moving From *Hierarchy* to *Harmony*

(A 9-WEEK BIBLE STUDY)

AMBER H. JONES

Copyright © 2018 by Amber H. Jones

All rights reserved. No part of this publication may be reproduced, distributed, or transmitted in any form or by any means, including photocopying, recording, or other electronic or mechanical methods, without the prior written permission of the publisher, except in the case of brief quotations embodied in critical reviews and certain other noncommercial uses permitted by copyright law. For permission requests, write to the publisher, addressed "Attention: Permissions Coordinator," at the address below.

Gold Digger Publishing, LLC
golddiggerpublications@gmail.com
www.amberhjones.com

Ordering Information:
Quantity sales. Special discounts are available on quantity purchases by corporations, associations, and others. For details, contact the author at the above email or website
for ordering.

Orders by U.S. trade bookstores and wholesalers. Amazon.com

Printed in the United States of America

Editing: Sarah Hayhurst

Design & Layout: Kelly Moroshan

ISBN 9781726628303
1. The main category of the book — Christian Books & Bibles, Bible Study
2. Other subject categories — Spiritual Growth, Women's Issues

First Edition

To Clayton the Brave, who journeyed alongside me as I worked through deep theology, deep emotions, deep doubt and, finally, deep joy. I love you.

To my writing group – Megan, Erin and Jen.
Your cheers, critiques and faith birthed this book.

To my children – Caleb, Taylor, Mari, Malia, Levi, Nya and Jude, who never seem to doubt that there's no limit to what I can accomplish. You give me wings.

To the One who created a seat for me – just for me – at His glorious family table and then invited me in to occupy it.
All that I am is Yours.

Contents

WEEK 1	Introduction	2
	Andrea's Story	10
WEEK 2	All Truth is God's Truth	12
WEEK 3	Subordinate and Defective	19
	Gavin and Fiona's Story	30
WEEK 4	The End was Only the Beginning	34
WEEK 5	The Lens of Christ	45
	James and Nora's Story	52
WEEK 6	Bible or Culture	55
	Lyla's Story	72
WEEK 7	Headship and Head Coverings	74
WEEK 8	Spiritual Gifting and Agency	88
	Patrick and Tessa's Story	101
WEEK 9	Harmony Restored	103
	Final Thoughts From the Author	125

A Seat at The Table

Introduction

There's something very wrong.

It's a common lament in circles of women, a not-so-well-kept secret alluded to at play dates and luncheons, Bible studies, and ladies' Christmas teas. It's the understood premise of so many women's conferences, self-help books, and mommy blogs.

We seem to intuit that there should be *more* to our walks with God, more to our purpose and place in the body of Christ, *more* to our lives at home. Like a maddening itch we can't scratch, we feel the rub of something not quite right but can't exactly put our fingers on it.

Instead, we strive to accept our places, our stations, our lots. We fill our calendars with women's events and acts of service at home, at church, and in our communities. We throw ourselves unreservedly into our children and our friendships and into bettering our marriages. With a distorted understanding of Proverbs 31 dangling over our heads, we chant to ourselves things like:

Live in the moment.

I'm the daughter of a king.

I'm worthy because God says I am.

Being a mommy is the most important job on earth.

This life should be satisfying.

Yet, we come back again to that feeling that something's missing, and far too often, we assume the problem lies within ourselves.

I've been there—sitting at yet another ladies' event aimed at encouraging women to exercise their gifts of homemaking and hospitality, lovemaking, and laundry, Sunday-school teaching, and kid chauffeuring—willing myself to pay attention, to be inspired, to get excited. I would invest the time and energy into events and books and gatherings with the theme of "biblical womanhood" only to walk away feeling further from God, ashamed of my inadequacies, and lackluster about Scripture, prayer, and most of all, gathering with my church family.

The messages were clear: A woman's place is in the home, tending to her family. When it comes to the church, there are significant limits to how, when, and where a woman can be of use, though the limits are often arbitrary and can vary from one house of worship to another.

In some churches women must remain silent, but in others they're allowed to encourage through worship. In one church, women can teach (as long as it's not with authority), while at another she must cover her head when she prays. Perhaps a woman can lead a boy, or even a teenager, in youth group; but when he crosses the threshold into manhood (an arbitrary date in itself), she would be considered out of order in some churches if she continued her ministry of discipleship. As convoluted as these scenarios sound, this is the reality of the plight of women in churches all over this country. From Sunday school to the altar of marriage, women are subtly and overtly taught that simply being female places them under limits that they can neither predict or overcome but that they must accept if they are to be right with their God.

Insolent Daughters of Eve

We're living in a pretty liberated time in history, especially in America. Women serve at every level of government, evidenced most recently when Hilary Clinton garnered the Democratic Party's nomination for President of the United States. The pay disparity between men and women is dwindling by the day. We enjoy equal rights with men in society, no longer beholden to our fathers, brothers, and husbands in terms of property ownership, entrepreneurial endeavors, and political activism. The holes in the proverbial glass ceiling are as exciting as they are numerous.

What's more, the power of the written and spoken word is now ours for the taking. We're no longer bound by silence, afraid to speak up when we're marginalized, abused, or overlooked. The recent #MeToo movement demonstrates that even if the social media

Complementarian

Male and female were created by God as equal in dignity, value, essence and human nature, but also distinct in role whereby the male was given the responsibility of loving authority over the female, and the female was to offer willing, glad-hearted and submissive assistance to the man.

(Christians for Biblical Equality)

format is all that is available, women are finding their voices and telling their stories whenever and however they see fit.

Yet, for Christian women in the American church, these liberties and equal footing are often checked at the doors of our homes and houses of worship.

Despite the biblical models for female leadership found throughout Scripture (Deborah, Esther, Mary Magdalene, Junia, and Phoebe to name a few) and despite the heavy presence of female teachers, preachers, and advisers found in the early church as well as throughout church history, the modern church continues to struggle with the idea that women are equally graced and possess equal capacities for the equipment of ministry as their brothers.

From Marcella and Paula, early church members who helped Jerome translate the Vulgate Bible and helped judge church disputes when he was away, to the mystics Julian of Norwich and Catherine of Siena, to the reformers Argula von Stauffer (Martine Luther's outspoken supporter, also referred to by enemies as the Insolent Daughter of Eve) and Katherine Zell, women have historically been entrusted with high ministerial callings and have executed their church duties with excellence and passion.

Even from its earliest inception, evangelicalism was carried forward by women and men alike, with leading Bible colleges such as Moody Bible Institute, Nyak, and Gordon College offering pastoral and evangelism training for females. Furthermore, several Methodist groups (Free Methodists, Wesleyan Methodists, and Church of the Nazarene) as well as Free Will Baptists, the C &MA, Quakers, and the Evangelical Free Church all either directly ordained women for ministry or strongly encouraged female leadership and equality at all levels of preaching and teaching ministry.

From the beginning, the debate was charged, but early evangelical proponents of biblical equality focused on creation-redemption in Christ as negating the curse from the fall and also on the liberating effects of Pentecost for all believers.

If the Spirit has been poured out on flesh—both men and women (Acts 2:18)—for the purposes of calling all people to the beauty of the gospel, who were they to limit women in ministerial calling?

Stay in Your Lane

The debate over whether women are capable, intelligent, strong, and effective has been, by and large, laid to rest in modern society. Yet theologians and laymen alike continue this dispute within the walls of church and academia, nevertheless.

Of course, one would be hard-pressed to find a minister alive who would put it that way. In fact, women are often praised from the pulpit and warmly acknowledged as important contributors to the ministry.

That is, as long as they stay in their lanes.

Somewhere along the way, probably due to a mixture of fearful backlash against secular feminism and a desire to adhere to a strict literal interpretation of the Bible, the culture in many churches began to shift backward in their admittance of women into preaching and teaching ministry.

The helping ministries, such as hospitality, church cleaning, and outreach, became the domains of women. Some churches kept women in staff positions of ministry to children, youth, and other ladies. Musically gifted women were utilized in worship ministry. Yet, they were prevented from preaching, teaching, and evangelism more and more often.

It's not uncommon today to attend the same contemporary worship service at the same church Sunday after Sunday and never hear a woman speak or even see her pass a communion plate.

The lanes are well defined even if they aren't well articulated. It may be uncouth, in this modern age, to discuss gender norms and biblical roles from the pulpit, but the lanes are there, nonetheless, perhaps written into church bylaws or simply unspoken rules that everyone seems to follow without question.

Here Begins Our Journey

Though Jesus seemed to turn cultural expectations on their head and often showed little regard for gender norms (and even propriety, e.g., Luke 7:36–50; John 8:1–11) and though he seemed to empower women for ministry (John 4:28; Luke 24:10), still the church struggles.

Though the early church was built by women and men working side-by-side in all the gifts of the Spirit and though, historically, women have held and excelled at prominent ministry positions, still the church grapples.

Though our society is moving on from systems of gender inequality and though the women, men, and children who sit in our pews are crying out for an end to the hierarchy that has robbed us of the voices of so many daughters of God, still the church debates.

In the era of #TimesUp and #MeToo, it could be said that the stakes have never been higher. We must get this right. We owe it to ourselves, our children, and our Lord to take a fresh look at the ancient and beautiful Word of God, to do diligence in parsing Scripture and synthesizing cultural information, and to emerge from earnest investigation with truth.

This study is designed to examine the big questions of women's roles in the church while also challenging you to thoroughly hash out the implications of several interpretations of Scripture.

The goal is not to convince you of any one viewpoint as much as it is to shed light on controversial passages, to provide often-forgotten cultural context, and to introduce alternative perspectives that aren't necessarily new but perhaps *new-to-you*.

We will dig into Scripture from creation to the resurrection of Christ and, when we get uncomfortable, we'll just dig in some more. My hope is that when we emerge together from this study, we will have a proper perspective of Scripture, as well as a newfound confidence and excitement for what life with the Holy Spirit can be like when all God's children get to take a seat at the table.

Egalitarianism

God created male and female as equal in all respects. Gen. 1:26-27 makes no distinction between woman and man insofar as both are equally made in His image (i.e., ontological equality), and both are given the responsibility to rule over His creation (i.e., functional equality).

(Christians for Biblical Equality)

Reflection & Discussion

1. There are essentially two views adopted by the church-at-large in regard to the differences between women and men in ministry. The first is complementarity, which avoids a hard-and-fast definition but, in essence, asserts that men are empowered and women are restricted in certain ways and for certain ministries, especially in leadership roles. The other view, known as egalitarianism, asserts that although differences exist between men and women, they do not do so to the extent that they are empowered differently for ministry. In other words, women and men may enjoy complete equality at church and at home.

   - In your experience, what roles have been restricted to women in the church? What differences in ministry have you observed between men and women?

     _____
     _____
     _____
     _____

   - Have you ever received explicit or implicit teaching that women are subordinated to men on the basis of gender alone? If so, what logic was used to defend that position?

     _____
     _____
     _____
     _____

2. Reflect on this quote by Charles H. Pridgeon:

   If it was "last days" on Pentecost, it certainly is now. Millions are perishing for the bread of life. If there is not only a present world that needs regeneration, but also a hereafter of heaven or hell, we who have the light can realize our awful responsibility. Our forces need to be mobilized and that not only of men but also women and children. The question of the ministry of women is more than just an academic question. The force of men who offer for His service is inadequate. Souls are perishing. There is not time to argue whether it be a man or woman that performs the service. The need must be met. The dying one that is saved will be saved just as well by whomsoever brings the Word of Life. We can split hairs, look wise, and hold up some possible meaning of a text or two of Scripture when the whole trend of God's Word is on the other side; millions are going to hell while we delay.

- What Scriptures have you studied or been exposed to that seem to suggest female subordination on the basis of gender alone?

  _____
  _____
  _____
  _____
  _____

- Consider, for a moment, that the "whole trend of God's Word" is, in fact, "on the other side" of complementarity. What implications does this have for church ministry? What would your own life look like if you knew this was true?

  _____
  _____
  _____
  _____
  _____

3. Spend time in prayer and contemplation. Ask the Lord to open your eyes and ears to the truth and to empower your mind and heart for the task ahead. Contemplate what drew you to Christ in the first place. What was it about Jesus that attracted your heart?

   _____
   _____
   _____
   _____
   _____

Andrea's Story

Andrea looked around her pastor's office as she waited for him to arrive for their scheduled meeting. Nervous and in need of distraction from the enormity of what was riding on this appointment, she read the inscriptions on the numerous plaques ornamenting the walls. He'd achieved so much in his lifetime—advanced degrees in theology and practical ministry, ordination, and honorary awards. She tried not to be intimidated, to remember that this was the same man who had baptized her at twelve and been to her parents' house for Sunday dinners on countless occasions, who had counseled her when she was grieving the loss of her grandmother, and who prayed for her when she was heartsick over her first break-up.

Through good times and bad, John Norris had been her pastor for her entire life. Her dreams were safe in his hands.

Pastor Norris opened the door and smiled in his usual broad and bright manner. Andrea tried to relax at the familiar sight, but something gave her hesitation. It was the look in his eyes. Did she see some sort of sadness there?

"Hi, Andrea," he said, extending his hand. A handshake? Usually, they greeted each other with a warm hug. She shook his hand and tried not to let the awkwardness she was feeling show on her face.

As Pastor Norris took his seat behind his desk, Andrea's stomach began to knot. His movements were stiff, and he wasn't making eye contact with her. Something was definitely wrong.

"I'm going to cut to the chase here, Andrea," he began, his eyes finally meeting hers. "I want to start by saying I've spoken to the elders about your internship application, and we're all proud of where your heart is in terms of your ultimate goals of working with the underprivileged in our city. That's the heart of God, and we believe in this kind of work."
Andrea straightened in her seat. Her entire body tensed as if braced for a blow.

"However, we have some pretty significant concerns," said Pastor Norris.

Andrea cleared her throat, and when she finally found her voice, the weakness in it was humiliating. "Concerns?" she asked.

Pastor Norris shifted in his chair. She realized he was uncomfortable, too.

"For starters, you're applying to seminary in the fall. You're requesting a pastoral recommendation, but, honestly, I can't give you that," said Pastor Norris. Our denomination is very clear on this—females cannot be ordained under any circumstances. You stated in your email that you're working toward ordination. We can't support that."

Her temples were throbbing, and she felt the heat rising in her face. Was she angry or embarrassed or both? She made a concerted effort to push aside her emotions. She'd *feel* things later.

Right now, she suddenly realized, any emotional reaction on her part could be perceived as weakness.

Andrea said, "Pastor Norris, did you read my email in its entirety? I've worked for four years to get into this seminary and this internship. I've put in the hours, academically and in ministry. I'm not seeking ordination for no reason. Ordination is absolutely necessary to complete the jobs God is calling me to do, sir." She'd never called him sir in the history of their relationship, but something had changed between them. He didn't seem like her ally anymore. She almost despaired to realize he was her superior. Her ministry was literally now in his hands.

"Andrea, I understand that this is a big disappointment," said Pastor Norris. "But did it occur to you to seek counsel from those God has placed in authority in your life before pursuing this path? The fact of the matter is that God can't be calling you into a ministry that requires you to lead men in any capacity. Ordination is reserved for male leadership because the Bible says that's the divine order of things. No matter how much we love you and believe in you, we can't go against what the Word of God says."

"So, you won't give me a recommendation?" said Andrea.

"No. We can't. I'm sorry, he said." He looked genuinely pained.

She sat for a long moment, allowing herself to absorb the shock. When Pastor Norris extended his hand again as he showed her to the door, she shook it weakly, any pretense of confidence and strength banished.

"I'm truly sorry, Andi. I know God will show you where you fit in the body of Christ. I'll be praying for you," he said with deep tenderness in his voice.

Andrea sat in her car, unable to even switch on the ignition. Her mind was racing, traveling backward to the first time she felt Jesus alive in her heart, to the first time she felt the leading of the Holy Spirit, to the moment she felt sure God was speaking to her about church planting in the inner city. She'd been working in soup kitchens, homeless shelters, and after-school programs for four years. When others ran from the pain and suffering so intertwined with those living in poverty, Andrea was compelled into it. The people she ministered to had become her family, her closest friends, her world. Their faces and stories were the fuel that kept her going during college when she switched her major to focus on a path toward seminary and ordination.

How could it have all been destroyed in the length of time it took to meet with Pastor Norris?

She'd been so sure of God's calling and of her giftings before her pastor entered the room, but now, for the first time, she was overwhelmed with doubt.

Did she get ahead of herself? Was it pride or naivety that had propelled her forward? Why hadn't Pastor Norris or her father, who was an elder at their church, spoken up during all her years of ministry? Why did the desire for ordination now negate everything?

The questions came pounding on the doors of her mind one after another until she began to cry.

Jesus, show me what to do.

Alone in her car, unsure of herself and her place in the world, she cried out to God.

All Truth Is God's Truth

You might say I wed them at once, Christ and my husband.

As a very young woman, I chose to love both of them for the rest of my life at around the same time. We began our early married days attending church every time the doors were opened, and during those years Christ was formed in both of us—His love, His presence, and His Word seeping deep down into our roots.

Because I was young and unchurched, I had developed no identity in Christ on my own before becoming *one* with someone else in covenant marriage. As you can imagine, it was nearly impossible to begin building the foundation of my own identity in Christ right away. After all, the tumults of a first-year marriage made learning to become a godly wife the urgent task at hand.

Therefore, I devoured every teaching, book, and piece of advice I could glean on the topic of biblical womanhood.

Not discipleship or sanctification.

Not holiness or equipment for ministry.

Not creation-redemption theology or eschatological perspectives.

I simply wanted to be a godly wife and, eventually, a godly mother. So, I bent myself toward this goal and studied, prayed, and talked about biblical womanhood with passion.

It's painfully obvious now, looking back. At the time, however, I couldn't see how very lopsided my theology was becoming and, therefore, how large were my blind-spots.

Complementarianism, or the traditional view as it is sometimes called, made absolute sense to me. Men and women were created differently and called to different tasks and ministries. Any woman who insisted that she partake in the prohibited ministry of teaching with authority was obviously greedy for the spotlight and discontent in the ministries to which she was called, usually those found in the home. *It wasn't that women were less than men*, I reasoned, they *were simply different*.

After a while, I became so certain of my complementarian viewpoints and so secure in my positions, that I began to speak with authority at Bible studies and debate others on the issue whenever the chance arrived.

Had I ever taken the time to objectively consider egalitarianism? No, I didn't see why I should expose myself to any alternative teachings when a plain reading of Scripture clearly laid out God's design for women as helpmeets, for female subordination in marriage and in the church, and for the prohibition of women in pulpit ministry.

I'll be eternally grateful for a self-proclaimed Christian feminist who challenged me on my viewpoints to the extent of finding the chinks in my complementarian armor that I never realized were there.

It was one simple question which sent my entire world into a tailspin: If we are to interpret all of Scripture literally and apply the principles/directives/advice found in the New Testament across all times and cultures, why do we not adhere to all of the principles/directives/advice in our churches today?

In other words, why are we cherry-picking?

I realized, after considering this question honestly and looking at the scriptural examples she provided, that I didn't have an answer to that question.

You see, I had based my entire life—my motherhood, my marriage, my very identity as a woman and a Christian—on a theological position that I hadn't fully vetted.

I hadn't done my homework and that realization terrified me.

Lovers of Truth

If you asked most Christians whether truth is important, they would probably look at you like you were as dumb as a bag of rocks and respond with, "Of course." Jesus is the way, the truth and the life (John 14:6), after all. The entire point of the gospel is that the truth has come down to us and is here to set us free (John 8:32).

Too often, however, Christians accept as truth teachings that have been passed down to them by way of tradition instead of coming to conclusions based upon vigorous study of their own. That's shocking when you consider what is at stake, but it's also reality.

Today, my friend, that will not be you and me. We are turning now to Scripture where we will begin by asking ourselves the hard questions of why truth matters and how we can arrive at truth rather than oppose it.

Let's open our Bibles up to John 4:23–24 and write these verses, in totality, below:

_____
_____
_____

The transliterated word for truth found in the New Testament 98 times is *aletheia*[1], which is rendered in the New Testament Greek Lexicon as "the truth as taught in the Christian religion, respecting God and the execution of his purposes through Christ, and respecting the duties of man, opposing alike to the superstitions of the Gentiles and the inventions of the Jews, and the corrupt opinions and precepts of false teachers even among Christians." It also is defined, objectively as "the true notions of God."

It's sometimes helpful to substitute the literal meaning of a word in place of its translated version in order to find the heart of what a passage is saying. Let's exercise this practice together by re-writing John 4:23–24, and each time the word truth is found, let's replace it with "the true notions of God."

How does this reading affect the way you experience this verse? Does it spark anything new in you? Provide any insight? Record your thoughts below.

_____
_____
_____
_____

Let's try this exercise again as we examine 1 John 1:6. Record the verse below and substitute "the true notions of God" for the word truth.

_____
_____
_____

Again, record 1 John 3:18–19 below in the same way.

_____
_____
_____

2 Timothy 2:15. Record it below using the same substitution.

_____
_____
_____
_____

By now, you're attuned to the point of this exercise. Many of us treat "truth" flippantly, arriving at conclusions with haste, never thinking twice about things that seem so obvious to our untrained eyes.

Yet, when you substitute that powerful phrase, "the true notions of God," into these familiar verses, a more serious chord is struck, isn't it?

God has notions. Notions are defined as "impulses or desires" or as "beliefs."

God, the Creator of your soul, the Author and Finisher of your faith, the Maker of heaven and earth has *desires, impulses, and beliefs* about the nature of things.

Let's bring that lofty concept to bear on the topic of this Bible study for a moment:

God—the Creator of women and men, of marriage, of family, and of the church—has desires, impulses, and beliefs about where every little, pig-tailed girl; every insecure, teenage young lady; every blushing bride; every tired mom; and every gray-haired grandmother fit into His plan, His church, and His world.

He has an opinion about whether or not women get a seat at the table.
I don't know about you, but that at once excites and unnerves me.

Consider that truth is more than a concept: that it is more like the "desires, impulses, and beliefs" of God. Describe how this makes you feel in regard to your approach to truth. Have you reverenced the truth as you should, or have you taken shortcuts in discerning it? How does it make you feel to consider God having an opinion on your place in the home and in church?

_____

_____

_____

_____

Once we accept that we may not have given the pursuit of truth its due, and once we realize that truth isn't just a concept but the very "notions" of God, we logically turn to Scripture to find truth. The problem arises, however, when we attempt to make broad theological assumptions based upon a few verses in the Bible.

The Breath of God

There are key passages in the Bible which deal directly with gender, with the roles of males and females at home and in the church, and with hierarchy in the body of Christ. It's customary for folks to play proof-text poker with one another when it comes to debating where Scripture stands on the issue of gender equality in the church.

"I see your 1 Timothy, chapter 2 and raise you a Hebrews 7:23–28!" You can almost hear them saying, eyebrows furrowed and voices low, in their best *Dirty Harry* impression.

However, the Bible is clear that the totality of Scripture is needed in order to arrive at the true notions of God. Record 2 Timothy 3:16–17 below.

_____

_____

_____

_____

Notice the words *all* and *breathed* and draw a big, fat circle around them because this is the heart of the matter, friend.

God doesn't just have notions stored in His infinitely complex mind, withholding them from us as he watches us twist in the wind on this peculiar planet.

He has done us the great honor of *breathing* his notions into a compilation of writings which have been painstakingly preserved and passed down to us throughout the generations. In your hand right now is at least some of the *very mind of God*. Doesn't it stand to reason that we should know and synthesize this truth as a whole?

When you consider cherry-picking pieces of other writings, the logic becomes clear.

For example, if I were to read a few key portions of *Gone with the Wind*, I could wrongly draw the conclusion that Scarlett O'Hara was a selfless, brave, industrious woman who loved her husband with ferocity.

If I were to read only snippets of the operational manual of my car, I could do severe damage to the machine.

The Bible is the most important manuscript in the history of human existence, and this is why cherry-picking verses and then applying them broadly to all cultures, across all time, and in all situations is serious business. This is not to suggest that the key verses relating directly to gender equality and roles should be ignored or dismissed.

The proper approach is to synthesize all of Scripture so that we may become "competent" and "equipped for every good work."

Now that we've established the importance of seeking after the "true notions of God" and that the entirety of Scripture is necessary for this task, we're ready to dig in further to the concept of biblical equality.

In the following chapters, we will begin to look at overarching themes in Scripture as well as the particular passages relating to males and females. It's an exciting prospect to know that every passage we study will be the notion of God, breathed into being so that we can live the abundant life!

Reflection & Discussion

1. I shared a personal story of how my eyes were opened to the inconsistency in my theology. Have you experienced anything like this? What were the results of your revelation?

   _____
   _____
   _____
   _____
   _____
   _____
   _____

2. Why is consistent theology important in terms of reaching the lost? What are some possible outcomes of an unchurched person joining a body of believers with inconsistent viewpoints about God?

   _____
   _____
   _____
   _____
   _____
   _____
   _____

3. Do you have any beliefs that are held in tension with one another? How comfortable are you with theological tension?

   _____
   _____
   _____
   _____
   _____
   _____
   _____

Subordinate and Defective

A full half of the body of Christ are simply inferior to the other half.

Women can't be entrusted with pulpit ministry or with most positions of authority.

Men, simply by being male, are better equipped and have received more divine authority on earth than their sisters in Christ.

Women are, at least on some level, defective and subordinate.

You'd probably never hear these stark statements spoken aloud in church, but the sentiments lurk there just the same, hovering over the pastor as he writes his sermons, over the elders as they make their judgments, and over councils as they write their bylaws.

When all the arguments are stripped down to their barest state, when all the moves in our games of proof-text poker have been exhausted, this is the bottom line.

The complementarian viewpoint espouses an "equal but different" hermeneutic, or interpretation, of Scripture. However, this description doesn't hold water when push finally comes to shove and the glaring question of why women are destined for subordination is, at last, asked.

Because God says so. That, essentially, is the uncomfortable and unsatisfying answer to this big question.

Does God, in fact, say that women are inherently inferior to men? Are women not only born with sin but also some sort of everlasting defect that prevents them from being fully equipped for ministry?

These are questions we absolutely must ask ourselves if we are going to structure our lives, families, and churches around this issue. In order to find the answers to the questions, we must begin at the beginning and examine creation, the fall, and the aftermath of sin in the world. However, it's imperative that we don't merely look at these passages with our human understanding. We must examine these concepts through the lens of Christ and the miracle of the cross.

In the Beginning: The First Account

God has graciously provided, through his divine breath, the beautiful account of creation found in the book of Genesis, chapter one. Let's take the time to record the words of Genesis 1:26–27 below.

_____

_____

_____

_____

_____

_____

_____

You may have read these words time and time again, to the point that they've become rote phrases. I encourage you to take this opportunity to look at this passage with fresh eyes, with the invigorating understanding that these words are God's notions about humanity—about you. With that in mind, go back and circle the word *mankind*. In Hebrew, this word is *adam* and is translated as man or mankind. Verse 27 contains the word man, which is translated from the Hebrew *ha-adam*.

Why is this important? Simply because verse 27 adds texture and provides the correct understanding of the word used in verse 26. Scripture is clearly referring to both males and females in this creation account.

According to verse 26, both males and females are equally created in the image of God. What does this passage describe as the purpose, or the manifestation, of this?

_____

_____

_____

_____

_____

_____

From these two verses, we may draw two conclusions: males and females are equally created in the image of God and at least part of the purpose of this "divine stamp" is so that they may "rule over," or order, the world *together*.

Let's now look at verse 28 of the same chapter. Record it below.

___

Circle the word blessed in the first sentence. This word, in Hebrew, is *barak*, and it can mean to praise, congratulate, or salute. Here we have the Creator of the world congratulating mankind on this brand-new, grand adventure to which he was calling them. Immediately following this salute, he gives them a few commands. List them, in your own words, below.

___

These commands follow a salute from the Creator God. This tells us that the shared responsibilities of males and females—of creating, of subduing, of ordering—were, from the very beginning, intended to be equal and joyful responsibilities of which both would partake.

What do you notice in these initial accounts of creation regarding equality between males and females?

_____
_____
_____
_____
_____

Do these verses suggest hierarchy between males and females or a relationship of harmony? How so? Give thought to this question and provide as many details in your observations as you can.

_____
_____
_____
_____
_____

In the Beginning: The Second Account

We've established some significant details of the creation account in the previous section, and now we're ready to move on to Genesis, Chapter 2 where the account is not contradicted but is enhanced.

Record Genesis 2:7 below.

_____
_____
_____
_____

Circle the word man again. Note that this time, the Hebrew word adam is accompanied by a definitive article which makes the translation "the man." In this account, the male is created first and alone and placed in a God-crafted garden.

Let's read Genesis 2:15. What is man's purpose in the garden?

_____

_____

_____

Directly after giving man the information and commandment regarding the Tree of the Knowledge of Good and Evil, God notes a problem and formulates a solution. Read verse 18 and record God's notions below.

_____

_____

_____

_____

Right of the First-Born

Verses 20–22 describe how God formed a suitable helper—the woman—by taking a rib from the man's side. Here's the juncture where equality is often called into question.

One of the main arguments for female subordination is based upon the order of creation. The argument goes like this: Man was created first, and he was given dominion over the earth. Woman was created second, clearly to be a helper to the man in his work. Therefore, males carry the authority that comes with seniority.

We still have on our "lens of Christ" so we could come up with all kinds of counterarguments at this point, such as the "upside-down" nature of the Kingdom of God in which the last become first and the first become last. Or we could venture off into the idea of primogeniture (the right of the firstborn to receive the inheritance) and how God repeatedly turned this cultural norm on its head in choosing the second, third, even last born of families to establish his chosen people on the earth.

Yet we don't have to go any further than a simple reading of the text, free of inferences of any kind. God created man from the earth and had a notion that it was not good for him to be alone. Therefore, being the ultimate problem solver, he formed a companion, a match to the set, if you will. Nowhere in Genesis 2 is there any indication that a hierarchical relationship exists, or should exist, between the man and the woman. This begs the question: what was the true nature of the relationship between them before sin entered the world?

1 Corinthians 11:11–12 provides a clue. Let's record it below.

_____
_____
_____
_____
_____

This passage clearly expresses the notion that man and woman are not independent of each other. The order of creation was not intended to demonstrate any kind of hierarchy, but to establish the need they have for each other.

In light of this, take a moment to consider whether patterns of gender hierarchy can support the notion of biblical dependence described in Genesis 2 and 1 Corinthians 11. What hierarchical relationships can you think of which model mutual, and equal, dependence? Record your thoughts below.

_____
_____
_____
_____
_____

The Powerful Name of Ezer

God decided that man should not be alone, so he made a helper for him. The word helper is translated from the Hebrew word *ezer*, [2] which literally means "helper corresponding to." Let's take a look at the man's reaction when he saw this *ezer* which God had taken from his own body. Record Genesis 2:23 below.

_____

_____

_____

_____

What feelings do you imagine the man was having as he beheld the woman? What parts of his exclamation give you this impression?

_____

_____

_____

_____

_____

One thing is obvious: the man recognized this new creature as the other half to a pair. "Bone of my bones and flesh of my flesh" suggest that it may have been like looking in a mirror or finding a long, lost twin you never knew you had.

Did the man make any assertions about the establishment of some sort of hierarchy? No. In fact, his response suggests the opposite—a complete equality of being between the woman and him.

Complementarians often assert that the word *ezer*, used to describe the female, denotes a subordinate position, and one of lending help to a leader. However, the word is used elsewhere in Scripture, often in reference to God. Let's look at these passages to provide some context.

In Genesis 49:25, Jacob blesses his sons, reminding them of the God who helps (*ezer*) them and the "Almighty, who blesses."

Exodus 18:4 finds Moses naming his son, Eliezer, for "My father's God was my helper (*ezer*); he saved me from the sword of Pharaoh."

---

[2] Strong, J. (1995). Enhanced Strong's Lexicon. Woodside Bible Fellowship.

Deuteronomy 13:7 is a plea from Moses on behalf of Judah, "Oh, be his help (ezer) against his foes!" and in verse 26 he describes God like so: "There is no one like the God of Jeshurun, who rides across the heavens to help (ezer) you on the clouds of his majesty." In verse 29, he continues "He is your shield and your helper (ezer) and your glorious sword."

A shield, a glorious sword, a savior, a rider of the heavens—this is our God and our *ezer*. What qualities come to mind when you read the verses above? Describe how you see God when you consider the fullness of what *ezer* means.

___

___

___

___

___

By now it's apparent that the description of the woman as *ezer* does not signify that she was some sort of assistant to the man, just as the Scriptures above do not indicate that God was merely an assistant to the humans he was helping. The woman was created to fill a deep need in the man and to share in the work, responsibilities, and enjoyment which accompany earth stewardship. The argument that *ezer* somehow indicates subordination fails miserably when we consider the fullness of the meaning of the word.

Naming and Claiming

Genesis 2:19–20 finds God forming the wild animals and the birds of the sky out of the ground. "He brought them to the man to see what he would name them; and whatever the man called each living creature, that was its name. So the man gave names to all the livestock, the birds in the sky and the wild animals."

Later, in verse 23, after the creation of the woman, the man said, "She shall be called woman, for she was taken out of man."

Proponents of female subordination assert that the fact that the man named the animals and then named Eve demonstrates that he was given authority over them both.

When a scientist discovers a new organism and gives it a name, does this signify the authority of the scientist over the organism? Likewise, what significance did the man's names have in the lives of the animals?

What is the purpose of the naming of things? Provide your thoughts in the space below.

_____
_____
_____
_____

For the man, the naming of the animals wasn't an exercise in authority. It was establishing a system of classification by which he could order creation.

His "naming" of the woman was a very different scenario. Previously, we recorded his reaction to the woman upon seeing her for the first time. He was nothing less than awed! He recognized her for what she was—something wholly different than the creatures he'd been classifying and trying to understand before. This creature was like him—bone of his bone, flesh of his flesh—and he called her after himself, the feminine form of the word by which God called him.

"She shall be called woman (*ishah*), because she was taken out of man (*ish*)" (Genesis 2:23).

Until this point, the word for man used in Scripture was *adam* (mankind) but, in this verse the word switches to *ish*, which literally means a man, and the woman is called *ishah*.

Far from implying some sort of hierarchy, *ish's* proclamation is one of astonished recognition of equality found in *ishah*. Instead of establishing a ladder of authority, this verse demonstrates two halves finally, and gloriously, becoming a whole once more!

Let's record Genesis 2:24 below.

_____
_____
_____
_____

> They become one flesh. This isn't the relationship of parent to child, of teacher to student, of soldier to superior officer. This is a relationship of complete, harmonious oneness.

The next chapter will delve into how the fall corrupted this relationship and perverted God's perfect design. However, we must never lose sight of God's true notions found in the first two chapters of Genesis.

- Man and woman were created equally in the image of God and given equal responsibilities and job descriptions.
- Harmony, not hierarchy, was established in both of the creation accounts.
- Man and woman are dependent upon one another to be fully human.
- Neither man nor woman were created with any defect or destiny of subordination

The final verse of Genesis 2 is almost painfully beautiful. Record verse 25 below.

___

It's painful because we look at this moment after having lived through the generations of brokenness, perversion, and dysfunction that have plagued humankind since then. The innocence of the man and woman, naked and without shame, is breathtaking.

Yet this is what we were meant for as a human race. Men and women—pastors and congregants, husbands and wives, sisters and brothers, friend and friend—are meant to stand before one another in complete vulnerability and without a shred of shame.

This was the grand notion of God as breathed to us in the creation accounts. This is what we'll carry with us as we venture into the darkness of the fall, when all was lost. With the "lens of Christ," however, we will view the horror with the cross splashed across every page and see how that just might change everything.

Reflection & Discussion

1. Have you witnessed males and females in relationships of mutual dependence in your church? In your home? Describe some of those occasions.

2. Have you ever personally experienced being devalued simply for being female or have you witnessed this happen to someone else? Describe your experience.

3. Consider that the woman was created fully equipped for every work on earth, just as the man. How does this affect the way you think of ministry work? What about domestic responsibilities?

4. Have you ever been uneasy with the attitude and/or official position of your church toward female subordination? If so, how did you handle it?

5. Shame. It's a poison to the human soul. Have you ever felt ashamed of your spiritual giftings or for a passion God has placed in your heart? Share your experience.

Gavin and Fiona's Stories

Gavin took another lackluster bite of pot roast as he surveyed his family around the dinner table. The children, Harry and Laura, were squabbling over something or other, as usual. Gavin began zoning out after about the third round of he-said/she-said. It wasn't that he didn't want to engage, it was just that he had so much on his mind that the petty arguments of his tweens didn't even make the short list of concerns. His wife of fifteen years, Fiona, inserted herself in between them when she could, but it was a losing battle and Gavin was sad to see the frustration mounting on her face. This didn't bode well for conversations between the two of them later on in the evening.

Every couple of minutes he felt Fiona's eyes on him. He knew the look well. She was wordlessly begging him to intervene and, when he failed to respond, she wordlessly voiced her disgust. Lately it had gotten to the point that he could hardly meet her eyes because he knew what he'd find there—disappointment and disdain.

"Gavin, do you have something you'd like to say about this?" Her strained voice jolted him into the moment, and he realized everyone was looking at him, waiting for him to come up with some magic solution. Resentment reared up so swiftly that he couldn't stop himself before he raised his voice.

"Stop this incessant bickering! I don't care whose fault it is! Just stop!"

He pushed away from the table and stalked off to the kitchen, leaving his family in silence.

Immediately, he was filled with regret. A part of him wanted to go back and apologize, but he knew the damage was already done.

Sometimes he felt like giving up. It was all too much. He was the sole breadwinner in the family, which was fine most of the time. Yet the stress of his job, combined with the burden of knowing all of their financial affairs were on his shoulders alone, wore on him.

All of that probably would have been bearable, though, if he didn't have the pressure at home and at church to contend with as well.

It seemed like every time he turned around Fiona was pestering him about the spiritual condition of their children—nightly Bible studies he should be leading, discipleship he should be giving, and words of wisdom which apparently should be pouring forth from his mouth like King Solomon.

"You're home with them, Fiona. Can't you do some of this? You have more time with them than I do," he once tried to reason.

"Gavin, you're the spiritual head of this home. You should be leading all of us. It won't work coming from me. We need you to be the head."

He heard it from the pulpit as well and at every men's group he attended: he was responsible for not only himself but for every person under his roof, too. If anything was out of order, it was his fault. If they weren't growing spiritually, it was because of some sort of shortcoming on his part.

Man up.

Take authority.

Be the head.

He heard these things so often that they reverberated through his brain when he was trying to sleep at night. The problem was that he wasn't some spiritual giant. He was just a man trying his best to follow Jesus. He didn't usually have words of wisdom, deep spiritual insights, or mini-sermons ready to go at the drop of a hat. He was struggling like everyone else.

Besides, Fiona was constantly reading the Word of God and attending seminars, Bible studies, and retreats. She memorized Scripture and consulted commentaries. The woman was a true prayer warrior and lived her faith authentically.

He longed to learn with her and discuss ideas with no expectation that he was going to lead anything.

He missed the deep conversations they had in college, when they were just two kids in love with Jesus and each other. Now the weight of what was expected of them both—he to lead and her to submit—seemed to be dragging their passion and their friendship down to something he didn't recognize any longer.

He longed to connect with his kids like he once did when they were little. Now, there seemed to always be some kind of agenda he had to bring to the table if he wanted to be the kind of leader they needed in the home.

What he really wanted was to be in a partnership with Fiona, to come home from work and be open about what he was feeling and to know that, sometimes, she'd hold him up if he were weak. He wanted to be a team in raising the kids, not adhering to rigid roles that neither of them really fit, but instead working together to build on each other's strengths and make up for each other's weaknesses. He wanted to explore God with Fiona, learning alongside her like they used to do, not being expected to come home with some kind of theological lesson ready every day.

He'd trade the final say-so in matters of theology and finances and the authority which accompanied his place as the head of the family for a restored relationship with his wife and kids any day.

He stepped out onto the back porch and listened to the crickets chirping for a few minutes.

Lord, I know what your Word says I must do and be as the head of my family. So, why am I so overwhelmed and unfulfilled? Help me, Lord, to be what you've created me to be.

The End Was Only the Beginning

From the gorgeous picture of man and woman cleaving to one another, naked and unashamed, we turn to Genesis, chapter 3, where the perfection of human-to-God and human-to-human relationship is shattered in a moment of time.

Before examining this passage, and the themes of the fall and the curse, it's crucial to keep in mind what we're carrying with us from previous study. Namely, we understand that God's Word is really his *breath* which whispers his *true notions* to us on every page. Therefore, as we examine the events surrounding the fall, we keep in mind that we're always searching for God's true beliefs about the nature of things. In order to keep a proper perspective on his true notions, we look through the "lens of Christ" alone. We don't accept anything at face value. We dig and wrestle and peer through that clarifying lens until everything comes into sharp focus at last.

We have go through this process, friend. There's too much at stake.

Since there was no hierarchy between man and woman prior to the fall, no authority given to either of them except to be caretakers of creation, it stands to reason that the ideas of power and subordination were the rotten fruits of humanity's fall. Let's begin in the first verses of Genesis 3 to unpack how these events unfolded.

Out of Eden

In the beginning verses of the chapter, we're introduced to the serpent, who is described as "more crafty than any of the wild animals the Lord God made" (v.1). He begins the interchange with the woman by asking a backhanded and assumptive question about whether or not they were allowed to eat of the trees in the garden.

Obviously, the serpent had received this information somehow, whether he heard it directly from God or through listening to the conversations of others with the knowledge.

Have you ever had someone begin a line of questioning in a similarly manipulative manner? Something like, "Did Barbara really say she couldn't come to your party because she had to work?"

It's nothing more than bait, and the idea is usually to insert some sort of insecurity or discontent where previously there was none. In this case, the woman fell for the bait and engaged the serpent in conversation.

She explains, in verse 2, God's provision and his warning—his true notions—that though they were free to eat from all of the trees, there was one tree off limits and that was for their own protection.

What did God say would happen to mankind if they ate—or even so much as touched—the Tree of the Knowledge of Good and Evil?

_____

_____

The serpent responds with what can only be described as indignation. He tells her that not only will they not die but that God is actually trying to prevent something else from happening—something extraordinary. Record verse 5 in the space below.

_____

_____

_____

_____

_____

You will be like God.

The irony of this statement is that the man and woman were already made in the image of God, fashioned to perfection out of his true notion of good. They were given the God-like vocation of creating, ordering, and subduing the perfect world, which was made for them and their God to commune.

Was there more than this? The woman began to use logic to rationalize her desire to find out: it looked appealing to the taste, and it might give her something that God had withheld. She took some of the fruit and ate it. "She also gave some to her husband, who was with her, and he ate it" (v. 6).

This, my friend, is where we will take a long pause to consider some of the arguments commonly heard in favor of female subordination.

According to many in the complementarian camp, the serpent was usurping God's designed order of authority by approaching the woman instead of the man. The assumption is that, if the serpent had approached the man instead of the woman, the trick may not have worked. In other words, the usurpation of authority by the woman and the serpent is what led to the fall. Indeed, authority was being usurped, but not that of the man's. The serpent was challenging the authority of God Almighty.

In your own words, describe what you imagine was the serpent's aim in approaching the woman with the question. Try to clear you mind of any previous teaching on this issue and engage with the text alone.

___

What is often implicit in the assumption that the man wouldn't have fallen for the serpent's schemes is the idea that the woman was more prone to deception. Defective. Inferior. Less competent. If the man were in the same situation, he may have done something differently.

However, this is certainly not accurate. The man would have made the same decision as the woman, and we know this *because he did*. In case we have any doubts, verse 6 clears it all up for us. Go back up a few paragraphs, to verse 6, and circle the words "her husband, who was with her." In six simple words, the arguments that the woman was usurping authority, was defective, and was more prone to deception than the man crumble beneath the weight of the understanding that *he was there*.

The woman's husband—bone of her bone and flesh of her flesh—was there with her in temptation. Indeed, the Lord had given the original command to the man. Record Genesis 2:16–17 below. Circle the words "the Lord God commanded the man." He stood there with his wife, having received the direct notions of God himself, and he still chose to eat of the fruit.

In your own words, describe what this information means to you.

___

The serpent hadn't completely lied to them. As most crafty liars do, he mixed lie and truth to make an intoxicating cocktail of destruction. Record verse 7 below.

___

Week 4: The End was Only the Beginning

_____

_____

_____

_____

Their eyes were opened and immediately they began to deny God's true notions. God had said that they were good. In their nakedness, in their oneness, in their harmony, and in their collaboration they were good. Shame was one of the many new evils that began, right away, to take God's true notions—his beliefs—and pervert them into something terrifying.

They took cover, first from one another, and then, in verse 8, from their Creator God. The Lord was "walking in the cool of the day" when the couple heard him and hid. When God asked where they were, the man responded with, "I heard you in the garden and I was afraid because I was naked; so I hid."

First shame and now fear was introduced to the humans made in the image of a God impervious to either. The Hebrew word for naked is *arom*[3] and has a deeper meaning than simply lack of clothes. It means "to be exposed."

The man and the woman realized they were exposed—nothing was hidden from the elements or from one another or from God, and they began immediately working to relieve the anxiety that came with this knowledge. Later, when they heard "the sound of the Lord God," they had already clothed themselves in meagerness and haste, yet they feared God because of their lingering exposure.

Arom

ay·rome

Hebrew Lexicon: To be exposed, naked, nakedness

Have you ever felt exposed to the degree that you experienced anxiety, shame, and fear? Describe at least one instance below.

_____
_____
_____
_____

What were your automatic responses to these feelings?

_____
_____
_____
_____

If you've experienced a traumatic exposure, you can relate to the man and woman. Already, the effects of sin were seeping into the relationships God had so lovingly designed. Where there was once harmony and oneness, now suspicious isolation seemed the safer option.

When God begins to question them, demanding to know what has happened, the couple enters completely unfamiliar territory. They begin to blame shift. First, the man blames the woman, while also insinuating it is God's fault for putting her there in the first place (v. 12). In a dramatic change of heart, the man, who previously exclaimed with astonished recognition at the sight of the miraculous mate God had provided for him, now insinuates that her very creation and presence is a pit into which he fell.

Take a moment to consider how quickly the man's heart changed toward the woman. Let his new and dark sentiments sink in. Describe, in your own words, the toll this kind of attitude could take on the man's relationship with God and his wife.

_____
_____
_____
_____

Then, the woman blames the serpent for deceiving her (v. 13). This is problematic for two main reasons: 1) The woman is denying her own logical processes. She's denying the fact that she deliberated before partaking of the fruit. Unlike her husband, who seemed to eat without reasoning first, the woman used her logical faculties before making her choice. 2) The woman, like the man, refuses to answer to the Lord with full honesty. She isn't owning her place in this tragedy or in history.

Consider how refusing to accept responsibility for not only your actions, but for your own spiritual condition, affects your relationship with God and others.

Now consider that complementarians believe the man is ultimately responsible for the spiritual leadership of his wife. In light of what we've just witnessed in the relationship of the man and woman, consider how this spiritual headship belief could be detrimental to the spiritual welfare of both men and women in the church. Provide any insights you have below.

___

___

___

___

The Lord hears them out and then issues the first of two curses. He curses the serpent to a life of crawling and dust-eating as well as eternal enmity between his offspring and the woman's (vv. 14–15).

Interestingly, when he addresses the woman, it is not with a curse. He describes what existence will now be like for her and her female descendants on the earth. Record what God says to the woman, in verse 16, below.

___

___

___

___

Two changes were to take place in the life of the woman: 1) She would bring forth life, and it would be severely painful and 2) She would desire her husband, and he would rule over her.

The Hebrew word for desire in this text is *teshuqah* and it can mean, roughly "desire to control" or, alternatively, "turning." The Septuagint, the Greek Old Testament, translates the word as *apostrophe*, which has several definitions but the only fitting one, in this context, is "when one turns away from all others to one person and addresses him specifically[4]. The preposition found in Genesis 3:16, toward, suggests that "turning" might also be a good fit for this verse.

Let's read that verse again, substituting desire to control for the word desire.

Your desire to control will be toward your husband, and he will rule over you.

What does this rendering suggest to you? Provide your thoughts below.

_____
_____
_____
_____

Now, let's read it again, substituting turning for the word desire.

Your turning will be toward your husband, and he will rule over you.

What does this rendering suggest to you? Provide your thoughts below.

_____
_____
_____
_____

Teshuquah

Hebrew Lexicon: Desire to control, turning

Apostrophe

Greek Lexicon: When one turns away from all others to one person and addresses him specifically

Either way this passage is rendered, the basic meaning is the same. Whether the woman desires to control her husband or she turns away from God and all others and turns toward her husband alone, she has moved into a broken relationship with him. The second part of that verse sounds the final death knoll as it describes the husband's resulting change toward her.

He will rule over you.

Thus, we get to zoom in on the fatal moment when patriarchy took root in the world. Proponents of hierarchy often point to this as the moment in time when God *prescribed* female subordination. The assumption is that the Creator God, whose notion it was to make two perfect halves of a glorious whole and place them in a perfect world so that they could co-create and co-order it, was so furious with their sin that he decided to permanently decree male dominance as the divine order of existence. This assumption makes sense when one is already carrying other assumptions, such as inherent female deficiency, created order primogeniture, and female fault in regard to being deceived by the serpent. Why shouldn't the woman—and all her female descendants across all of time and space—have to pay a hefty penalty for her weakness?

> When those assumptions are stripped away, however, this passage becomes, simply and terribly, a description of what existence would become for the woman. God is giving the woman a dire warning about the results of her choice.

Before delving deeper into that topic, let's take a look at the fate of the man. In verse 17, God says to the man, "Because you listened to your wife and ate fruit from the tree about which I commanded you, 'You must not eat from it,' Cursed is the ground because of you; through painful toil you will eat food from it all the days of your life. It will produce thorns and thistles for you, and you will eat the plants of the field."

This is the second curse God pronounces. First, he cursed the serpent and now he curses the land. No longer will the man lead a life of ease and comfort. Life is now going to be about survival. The land would make sure of it.

Notice that God does not capitulate to the man's insinuation that the wife God gave him was to blame for this situation. Indeed, God holds the man's own feet to the fire with two simple words. Go back up to verse 17 and circle the words "you listened."

The man is responsible for his own actions and will suffer similarly to the woman. Both are doomed to a life of pain, hardship, and laboring for survival alone.

Record verse 19 in the space below.

_____
_____
_____
_____
_____

> Here was God's dire warning to Adam. Death had entered the world. After a life of struggle, the man would return to the dust from which he came.

The man calls his wife, for the first time, by a formal name. Below is the literal Hebrew reading of verse 20.

"Now the man called (out to) his wife (ishah) a name (a mark or memorial of individuality; by implication honor, authority, character) Eve (Chavvah – life giver) because she was the mother of all living."

Again, much has been made by the complementarian camp about the man naming the woman. When assumptions aren't carried into the interpretation, however, it becomes clear that the man is, once again, recognizing something in his wife and calling it out. The man, at this juncture, is not in the position of naming and claiming authority. He has just been cosmically demoted, humbled beyond what you or I could ever imagine. He is simply calling out Eve for what *God has now made her become*—life giver.

Before we leave Genesis 3, it's important to note that after God lovingly clothed the couple, he said something remarkable in verse 22. Record it below.

_____
_____
_____
_____
_____

Apparently, the man and woman had been eating of the tree of life prior to the fall. Now that they had partaken of the Tree of the Knowledge of Good and Evil, and everything had changed, God was going to have to make sure they could no longer live forever. Two very important questions emerge at this point.

1. What, exactly, had changed since the man and woman ate of the forbidden fruit? Be as precise as you can in answering this question below.

_____
_____
_____
_____

2. Why would God not want the couple to live forever now that things had changed so drastically?

_____
_____
_____

It's crystal clear, isn't it? What had changed is that the perfect communion and intimacy between humanity and God was fractured. Furthermore, the collaboration, harmony, intimacy, and oneness between humans was shattered beyond repair. What was left was a bleak world of hard labor, power struggles, misplaced desires, and hopelessness.

God would not allow this to go on forever. He would make sure that the man and woman did not live for eternity in this pathetic state. He was going to prevent them from what he knew fear would drive them to do: grasp onto this hopeless way of being forever because they were scared.

So, he banished them from the garden and immediately implemented what would become his grand rescue plan. They didn't realize it then, but sin and all the aftermath of their terrible choice would not be the final word in God's story. The end was only the beginning.

Reflection & Discussion

1. Have you been exposed to teaching which ascribed special blame to the woman for the fall of mankind? What was the logic used?

   _____
   _____
   _____
   _____
   _____
   _____
   _____

2. Consider that a woman's femaleness is an inextricable part of her humanity. In other words, she cannot be human any other way. Imagine a picture of a female human. Now, lay on top of that picture the transparent film of the notion that there was, from the beginning, something deficient in the female. She was created deficiently so as to need the authority and leadership of her husband. Now lay on top of the picture of the female another transparent film. This one is the notion that the woman fell even further from perfection, further down the ladder of entrusted authority, after the fall of mankind. What you had before the layovers, was the picture of a female human, created in the image of God. What you have after the layovers is something less than that. Take a moment to consider the ways that female subordination cuts to the root of female humanity. The church rejects the idea that humans of color are deficient because of the inextricable aspect of their humanity that is the color of their skin. How does this speak to the issue of female subordination?

   _____
   _____
   _____
   _____
   _____
   _____
   _____

3. Think about the indisputable effects of hierarchy. By its very definition, it creates space between two people. In the military, superior officers can lose their jobs for fraternizing with their subordinates. Likewise, parents keep space around the "adults-only" parts of their lives. Similarly, teachers keep distance from their students. We understand and accept that this is a part of how hierarchical systems must function if they're to do so properly. Now juxtapose this understanding next to oneness a married couple is supposed to experience. Also consider the oneness that every member of the body of Christ is supposed to experience (John 17:20–21). How can hierarchy based upon gender exist together in a church or marriage of perfect oneness?

_____
_____
_____
_____
_____
_____

4. Discuss whether hierarchy lends itself to harmony or suspicious isolation.

5. "All that was lost in Eden was gained back at Gethsemane." What a powerful gospel message! Discuss this statement and its implications for female subordination.

The Lens of Christ

The difference between *prescription* and *description* is of the utmost importance when reading all of Scripture. For instance, numerous passages exist which describe polygamy, slavery, adultery, murder, and a host of other grotesque evils. It's improper to assume that, because something is described, that it is also condoned or *prescribed* by God. For instance, part of God's warning to the man included the prediction that the earth would "produce thorns and thistles" for him. Is this text describing what the earth would become, or is it prescribing that thorns and thistles are now God's ordained design, thereby prohibiting any circumvention? In other words, is using weed killer or agricultural technology tantamount to perverting God's design for the world?

The earth is cursed, but, as Christians, are we to passively accept all of the aftermath of the fall?

Consider these questions as we move forward with this idea of redemption.

As we've seen in Genesis 1 and 2, God created the first marriage and designed it for two people, male and female. Yet, as early as Genesis 4, we see polygamy crop up in the case of Lamech, a descendant of Cain. Though the Bible records Abraham taking a second wife for himself, the aftermath of this disastrous decision is described as well. Polygamy is not God's design or his will for human marriage, and virtually all modern-day Protestants and Catholics agree. Yet God's breath—his Word—doesn't directly address or condemn Abraham or Lamech for their severe shift away from his true notions. He allows the sad story of sin to play out, as it will, until the day when Christ enters human history.

Let's go a step further and examine what the New Testament has to say about slavery. In Ephesians 6:5, Paul gives a *prescription* to slaves when he tells them to "obey your earthly masters with respect and fear, and with sincerity of heart, just as you would obey Christ." This, at face value, seems to mean that slavery is not only condoned by God, but that the enslaved Christian must live out her captivity with her whole heart.

Yet, in 1 Timothy 1:10, Paul lists the slave trade alongside a host of other ghastly evils that are "contrary to the sound doctrine that conforms to the gospel concerning the glory of the blessed God." He also encourages slave owners to set their slaves free (Philemon 16), to view their slaves as equal (Galatians 3:28 and Ephesians 6:9) and, finally, exhorts slaves to win their freedom if they can (1 Corinthians 7:21).

Here we have several different passages, many of them prescriptive, that seem to contradict. How is this possible? If the Bible represents the true notions of God, how can it at once condemn slavery and also make provisions for it?

This is where a redemption hermeneutic, or the "lens of Christ," is especially necessary.

The other option, viewing these slavery Scriptures with a static hermeneutic, will necessitate that we, as Christians, not only accept slavery but that we encourage those who are enslaved to be the best slaves they can be!

Obviously, the modern church rejects this idea in totality. Christians have always been, and continue to be, on the forefront of anti-slavery movements. How do we reconcile our apparent departure from the prescription of Ephesians 6:5? By acknowledging that we are part of God's redemptive movement on this earth, called to be salt and light, a beacon on a hill. We understand, based upon the totality of God's Word, that the enslavement of human beings is antithetical to God's true notions. Therefore, we have no problem gleaning what we can from the heart of Paul's directive in Ephesians 6:5 (to yield ourselves to the obedience of Christ in whatever situation we find ourselves in) and moving on with God's ultimate story of redemption.

In other words, we read this passage, and others, with the lens of Christ over our eyes. This enables us to move beyond a bound-in-time application of every text, while still staying true to the crux of Scripture. Yet, when it comes to female subordination, complementarians pick and choose when to look through that precious lens and when to put it down, in the name of a "high view of Scripture." Let's take a look at some of those instances, beginning with 1 Peter 3:5–6. Record the verses below.

_____
_____
_____
_____
_____
_____
_____

Most hierarchicalists do not propose that this passage should be taken to mean that women should refer to their husbands as "master/lord." Modern-day churches, even conservative ones, see that God's true notion here is that women should not be afraid of being perceived as unbeautiful or plain, doing all that they can to adorn themselves to achieve a cultural beauty status. Rather, as long as they "do what is right," they will be like the daughters of faithful Sarah. Without realizing it, then, many complementarians are viewing this passage through the lens of Christ, which is leading them to a redemptive-movement interpretation.

Let's now look at 1 Corinthians 14:34. Record the verse below.

_____

_____

_____

_____

_____

This is one of the straightforward prescriptive verses that tease apart the inconsistency of non-egalitarian logic. Here we have Paul saying that women are to be silenced in church. Yet, most churches, even highly complementarian ones, allow women to sing, pray, make announcements, and even read Holy Scripture. Why is this Scripture not held up as the standard for women's roles in the church?

In order to understand how we can seemingly ignore biblical prescription, we must read more than this one verse. Preferably, we would give the entire book of 1 Corinthians a thorough reading and deep study. This would provide us much needed context for the book as a whole. For the purposes of this current study, however, we will only read chapter 14. Take a moment now to read the entire chapter, making notes below of anything that stands out to you, especially overarching themes or clues as to what the verse at hand might really mean.

_____

_____

_____

_____

_____

I don't know about you, but verses 26–33 are highly confusing to me when read right before verses 34 and 35. On the one hand, "sisters" are included in the category "each of you" who are then exhorted to come together with hymns, words of instruction, revelations, and tongues or interpretations. On the other hand, women are to "remain silent in the churches." One thing is for sure, though, Paul cannot possibly be talking about "hymns, words of instruction, revelations, or tongues/interpretations" when he is commanding the women to be silent.

In other words, this is a particular silence for which he is calling. Verse 35 lends us the clue we need to understand the kind of silence Paul is commanding. "If they want to inquire about something, they should ask their own husbands at home; for it is disgraceful for a woman to speak in the church."

Apparently, women were asking questions in church. This was not an uncommon practice for men to do in Jewish or Greek learning environments. However, not just any common Joe off the street could wander in and start asking questions. There was a propriety to the learning environment that included the student having some educational background on the subject at hand before asking questions.

Jewish boys generally received extensive education in Torah (the Old Testament), but the same was not true for girls. Likewise, Greek women received little, to no, education aside from training in household duties. Therefore, most of the women in the early church were uneducated and hearing this gospel of freedom for the first time.

They had questions and wanted answers. Unfortunately, they were disrupting the assembly and order needed to be restored.

Keep in mind, as well, that the same Paul who commended the entire Roman church to "our sister Phoebe, a deacon" (Romans 16:1), wrote 1 Corinthians 14:34. Record verse Romans 16:2 below and then consider its meaning alongside the Corinthians verse. Provide your thoughts after you record the verse.

_____

_____

_____

_____

_____

Likewise, turn to Philippians 4:2 and record it below. After you record it, circle the words "contended at my side."

_____

_____

_____

_____

Here, the very same Paul is listing two women, Euodia and Syntyche, as his co-workers (remind you of Edenic imagery?) along with their male counterpart Clement (v. 3) in laboring for the gospel. Paul's perspective here seems to be one of complete equality between the male and female members of his cohort. There isn't the slightest hint of segregation or subordination in these verses.

This is why most modern-day churches do not take 1 Corinthians 14:34 to be a bound-in-time prescriptive and so allow women to speak, at least in some form, in church. They are using a redemptive-movement interpretation, combined with a contextual and cultural understanding of this passage, to arrive at a more relaxed stance on women speaking in church. This, my friend, is an example of reading Scripture through the lens of Christ and should not only be applied when our biases allow or when it is more convenient.

The lens should be on our eyes at all times, eagerly looking for Christ's corrections on every page.

Reflection & Discussion

1. How is inconsistent interpretation of Scripture dangerous?

   _____
   _____
   _____
   _____
   _____

2. As mentioned in the introduction, many women in the modern church have a sense that something isn't quite right with the application of Scripture to gender roles and norms, and yet they continue living under inconsistent interpretations and applications that have far-reaching effects on their identities, lives, and ministries. Why do you think this is the case?

   _____
   _____
   _____
   _____
   _____
   _____
   _____
   _____

3. Describe a time where you thought you were right about a passage of Scripture or a theological viewpoint only to change your mind later. What led you to this change?

   _____
   _____
   _____
   _____
   _____

4. American women are living in a time unparalleled in human history in terms of rights, privileges, educational opportunities, job choice, earning potential, and a host of other quality-of-life improvements. Compare the educational levels to modern women in the church with the women of the early church. What implications do you think progress has made on women's abilities to understand and synthesize Scripture as well as to teach and preach?

_____
_____
_____
_____
_____
_____
_____
_____

5. If the issue of female prohibition isn't about ability or educational level, and if the Bible—breath of God—makes clear that women taught, co-labored, served as deacons, prophesied, gave words of instruction, and, in general, operated in all of the gifts of the Spirit, what is the issue with women teaching and preaching today?

_____
_____
_____
_____
_____
_____
_____
_____

Nora and James's Story

"I don't think I can do this anymore," Nora said as she poured another cup of coffee. This was her third cup of the morning, unusual for her. The problem was that she didn't want to get dressed for church, so she kept pouring coffee and finding things to do around the house.

James sighed. "First our married couples' group and then you began to slack off on the women's Bible study. Now you don't want to go to church at all?" The exasperation dripped from his voice.

Until a year ago, Nora and James were a power couple. They'd met in grad school and earned their MBAs together, marrying right after graduation. They each landed great jobs and entered the life of which they'd always dreamed—successful, busy, financially sound, and free to pursue their passion of travel. They had it all.

After a few years of living the dream, they were both disillusioned. The life they'd built wasn't fulfilling anymore. Their luxury home seemed empty, their hobbies had become boring, their jobs more demanding, and their marriage had taken severe hits as a result.

They went to church one Sunday morning as sort of a last-ditch effort to find what was missing. The next step would have probably been divorce.

They'd researched churches online and chose Open Door Community Church because it seemed well-run, staffed with educated folks, and welcoming of newcomers. They hadn't been disappointed after their first visit. In fact, one visit turned into two and then three and, before they knew it, they were both walking down the aisle one Sunday morning to receive Christ as the Lord of their lives.

Over the past year, they'd been embraced by the body of Christ at Open Door. They were welcomed into the fold and discipled. They'd eagerly joined every class the church offered and jumped into every service project and event that they could. In many ways, they'd grown closer as a couple, and they could see a meaningful future together again.

A few months into their new journey, they'd both began to notice the attitude the church held toward women. Comments were made from the pulpit regarding the duty of women to submit to male authority. This made no sense to either of them, coming from unchurched backgrounds, but they shrugged it off because these people seemed so happy and loving. Maybe they held some old-fashioned beliefs, they reasoned, but that could be overlooked in light of all the good these folks had to offer.

Then they joined a married couples' small group, hoping to repair some of the damage that had been done between them and to find new ways of relating as Christian husband and wife.

It only took a few meetings before they were deeply disturbed by what they were hearing.

The materials they were reading seemed to suggest that the husband had the final say in all important matters in the household and that women were somehow deficient when it came to leadership in the home and the church.

To make matters worse, Nora began to get close to the wives in the group and heard chilling stories of husbands addicted to porn and wives struggling to choke down their opinions on matters of importance to themselves and their children, as well as depressed women who weren't finding any fulfillment as stay-at-home moms but whose husbands forbid them to work.

James, too, was disturbed at the level of disrespect he heard coming from the men in the group when they talked about their wives.

They made jokes at their expenses and even mocked the women's emotions as something petty and difficult to endure. On more than one occasion, he left feeling a little angry and out of place as some of the guys insinuated that he wasn't "taking charge" enough in his household.

"You wouldn't have a lot of these problems with Nora if you took your place as the leader," one brother had remarked after James poured his heart out.

When Nora suggested withdrawing from the group, James didn't protest. She was only verbalizing what he felt anyway. They dropped out, citing work conflicts, and hoped that would be the end of their involvement with whatever weird philosophy was floating around in some of the circles at church.

However, Nora came home dejected after joining a weekly women's Bible study, too.

"They're saying some of the same stuff," she said, almost in tears at dinner.

"Like what?" he asked though he was bracing himself to hear the answer.

"One of them suggested that I should have gotten pregnant by now and that I should consider if my career was really in line with what God wants for my life. Another lady mentioned that my role was mainly to support you in your goals and that my focus on my own goals might be what's robbing me of joy."

"How do they know that your career isn't what God wants for your life?" he asked, incredulous.

"That's just it! Apparently, the Bible says I am meant to run my household and support you in ministry and in life. This is what I was created to do, they say."

"Run our household? You aren't domestically inclined at all," he said.
She shot him a look, and he smiled sheepishly. "Sorry, honey, but you know it's true. I didn't marry you for your cooking and cleaning skills," he said.

"Exactly! That's not who I am at all. Yet after I leave Bible study each week, I wonder if there's something wrong with me. Every woman there either stays at home or wishes she could. Their ministries are mainly toward their families and other women. I have no desire to do any of that. I was hoping I could be of service to Jesus with the talents I have, but it seems like I don't fit in anywhere," she said. It had been a few months since that conversation, and things had only grown worse. Now Nora didn't even want to go to church most Sundays. In all honesty, James didn't either.

They'd come to Christ because they needed purpose and hope.

They'd received both of those things at first, but now it felt like they were being taken away. They didn't want to be forced into prescribed gender roles and stereotypes. They just wanted to be salt and light in their workplaces and to build a strong marriage that would equip them for whatever ministry might be on the horizon.

"Dropping out of church can't be the answer," he said. He pulled her close into a deep hug.

"Are all churches like this?" she asked.

He could feel her tears soaking his shirt. Hot anger flashed within him. "I don't know," he said.

"I hope not," she cried.

He held her closer, confused and hurt and angry. "We don't have to go, honey. It'll be okay." He closed his eyes and prayed silently that it really would be okay.

Bible or Culture?

One of the chief concerns of the evangelical church in the last few decades has been the so-called "culture war" waged against Christians by the secular world. From abortion to same-sex marriage to the legalization of marijuana, the position of the church-at-large has been at odds with that of the culture-at-large.

The growing vocalization surrounding women's issues by the culture, as seen in the #MeToo movement, is only the newest of several feminist agendas which have challenged the church's stances on women's roles and rights. The result has been to deepen the suspicion that egalitarians are really no more than secular feminists in disguise, subversively spreading an anti-family, anti-traditional sentiment throughout the church. Thus, to suggest that a thorough reconsideration of our hermeneutical approach is in order on the issue of women's roles is tantamount to declaring yet another culture war on tradition and family values in the eyes of some complementarians.

Culture is defined as the "set of shared attitudes, values, goals, and practices that characterizes an institution or organization."

When Christians complain of a culture war, they usually mean that their values and way of life are being threatened. This begs the question: from where do Christians get their cultural norms and values?

The natural response from most Christ followers would be, "From the Bible, of course." Yet, have we reviewed what the Bible has to say about gender roles and norms? Have we examined the bound-in-time culture from which the New Testament writers were penning the sacred words, enough to differentiate between what was a cultural provision and what was at the "timeless heart" of the Scripture? Have we compared and contrasted our current culture with the Greco-Roman culture for the purpose of ensuring that our "literal" adherence to particular verses will achieve the same goal as it would have thousands of years ago in a completely different period of history?

A Tortured Hermeneutic

Is the subordination of women—a full half of the Body of Christ—God's true notion of what is *good* in terms of the shared attitudes, values, goals, and practices that characterize his family?

Because, if it is, then we must embrace female subordination fully. We must resist ignoring those Scriptures that seem to prescribe the role of women to be that of long-haired, silent learners, completely plain and humble in appearance, dedicated to homemaking alone, and submissive to every male in the church.

We must stop picking and choosing those bound-in-time verses we feel comfortable enforcing and, instead, live by them all.

However, if we understand that *Scripture interprets Scripture*, that God spoke His eternal word in historically particular circumstances and through various literary genres, then we know that we must interpret all Scripture through the redemptive hermeneutic—the lens of Christ—in order to ascertain his true notions. With this in mind, we can read Paul's directives to the churches of Corinth and Ephesus and understand that some of what he is instructing will not be applicable to our time and place in history, while *all* of the "heart" of what he's saying is timeless.

Unfortunately, what most churches have going on is more of what theologian Gordon Fee calls a "tortured hermeneutic." On the one hand, a high view of Scripture demands that we interpret each verse literally and apply it fully; on the other hand, applying certain verses is either impossible or problematic, so we politely ignore them and hope no one asks why. This is how we find churches allowing women to pray and sing but not to teach or preach. This same tortured hermeneutic is how we find marriages in which both partners want to be engaged in spiritual growth and important life decisions, but it's left to the husband alone to spear-head these things for the entire household. In truth, many complementarian marriages are so in name only. The church's interpretations of male headship and authority are so out-of-touch with practical life in American society that they are rarely applied in total.

In order to understand God's true notions in some of the challenging passages regarding women and the church, we will need to zoom out to get a macro view of the author, the audience, and the main points of the book in which the passage-at-hand is found. Then we will juxtapose the verse with what we know of God's notions elsewhere in Scripture. We will ask ourselves, again and again, two things: *What is the intention here? What does the text mean as an eternal word for us?*

After synthesizing this information, we will hopefully arrive at a deeper understanding of these verses, which have caused so much division in the church.

1 Timothy

The often-debated passages in 1 Timothy are parts of a larger writing in which Paul voices deep concerns with a few issues in the Ephesian church. Take a few moments to read all of 1 Timothy from start t o finish. As you read, answer the following questions:

1. Who was Paul writing to and why?

_____

_____

2. What theme occurs over and over again?

_____

_____

3. What are some of the sinful behaviors Paul is seeking to correct? List as many as you notice.

_____

_____

_____

_____

The Ephesian church, *a particular church body in a particular setting at a particular time in history*, was experiencing disputes, false teachings, and disruptions in family life and congregational order, among other things. As we discussed previously, women were using their newfound freedom in Christ to apparently disrupt congregational teachings. Let's examine 1 Timothy 1:6. Record it below.

_____

_____

_____

_____

Though this verse isn't directly addressing women, it can be inferred from verses 11–12 that women being vocal in the congregation was a concern. Let's examine verses 8–15 a little closer. Since this passage is highly important to biblical equality, I ask that you write out verses 8–15 below. We will refer back to this passage many times, so it is important that we go slowly and immerse ourselves in these words.

_____
_____
_____
_____
_____

Let's begin with verses 9–10, where Paul addresses female wardrobe. Go back up and circle the words "I also want" in verse 9. These words make all the difference in the world, don't they? Here, Paul is clearly stating that he wants women to dress in this certain fashion. This is a desire, not from God, but from Paul, as the founder of the Ephesian church. Take a moment to reflect on that and write down the impact this has on your opinion of the directive that follows.

_____
_____
_____
_____

According to Paul, why did he want the women to dress "modestly, with decency and propriety"?

_____
_____
_____
_____
_____

As a parent gives advice to a child or as the CEO gives directives to her employees, Paul is outlining the conduct *he* wants for the *Ephesian* church. He has reasons for asking that they dress a certain way—so that what will be noticed about the Christian women is their good deeds and not their wardrobe.

Who do you think Paul is concerned with showing "good deeds"? Why do you think he wants the women's actions to shine through?

___

Again, much like a parent who is seeking to apply God's notions to family life through the creation and enforcement of certain rules befitting their particular family's household, Paul is seeking to create and enforce appropriate guidelines befitting this particular church family. Another way of looking at this verse (and others like it) is this:

The "heart" of the verse – God's true notions

The application of the heart of the verse – Paul's discernment for a particular people, place, and time

After considering Paul's audience and his purpose, what do you think might be the bound-in-time portion of these verses?

___

What do you think is the "timeless heart" of these verses—God's true notions?

___

As mentioned in the previous chapter, the Greco-Roman culture was significantly different than that of modern America. "Elaborate hairstyles," gold, pearls, and expensive clothes could have signified a few things in that culture, among which are prostitution and/or higher status in society. Even today, expensive clothes and jewelry are status symbols all over the world. Paul's concern was that these new Christians were flaunting their status and/or their physical and material attributes to the world and perhaps even lording it over those of lesser status in the church.

In other words, this was a heart issue. Paul was dealing with a particular manifestation of a common human flaw—pride. This is widely understood by the evangelical church, which is why very few denominations police women's hairstyles, jewelry choices, and the cost of their clothing. Obviously, the audience to whom Paul is writing understood what he meant by "elaborate" and "expensive." However, modern-day application is problematic for us because those terms are subjective.

What problems can you foresee if a "high view of Scripture" requires us to apply this verse literally in our congregations today?

_____

_____

_____

_____

_____

How can we apply the "timeless heart" of these verses to our lives and our churches, even without policing the wardrobes of women?

_____

_____

_____

Let's now turn to one of the most controversial passages found in Scripture, verses 11–15. Go up and circle the words "I do not permit" in verse 11. Paul is laying out what he doesn't permit in the *Ephesian* church. This is the point where we'll turn to other passages to juxtapose them against this important one. Turn to Romans 16:7 and record it below.

_____

_____

_____

_____

Here we have a female apostle, Junia, which Paul is paying the incredibly high compliment of being "outstanding among the apostles." Apostles were more than simply teachers: they were disciples devoted to the purpose of itinerant teaching and preaching of the gospel. They established churches as they went along. In other words, they were Paul's contemporaries. *The same Paul who does not permit women to teach in the Ephesian church is publicly praising a female fellow apostle for doing just that.*

Let's now look at Romans 16:1–2. Write the verses out below.

_____
_____
_____
_____
_____

In these verses, the same Paul is commending the entire church in Rome to "our sister Phoebe, a deacon in the church in Cenchreae." He is establishing her as a leader and asks the church to give her whatever help she needs, calling her a "benefactor of many people, including me." Moreover, Phoebe is a deacon, or a teacher and leader in the church!

Directly following this, in Romans 16:3, Paul sends a greeting to another woman. Record verses 3–4 below.

_____
_____
_____
_____

Not only is Priscilla listed before her husband (that says something in and of itself), but Paul refers to her and her husband as his "coworkers." This term beckons us back to the harmony established between man and woman in the garden of Eden. Priscilla was a female working alongside her husband and the apostle Paul in the ministry. Verse 5 of Romans 16 says that they had a church which met in their home. Notice Paul is not addressing Aquila alone or referring to the church as his. *The same Paul who does not permit women to teach in Ephesus considers Priscilla to be a fully contributing ministry partner to the church in Rome.*

Consider what I mentioned earlier about Scripture interpreting Scripture. Now consider that Paul addresses women in a completely different manner in Rome verses in Ephesus. What does this mean to you?

_____
_____
_____
_____

Week 6: Bible or Culture?

We've established that Paul was giving a bound-in-time prescription to a particular group of people in time and location. However, an examination of 1 Timothy 6:1–5 will underscore this point more fully. Keep in mind that this is the same letter Paul has been writing all along. These are his instructions to the Ephesian church. Record verses 1–5 below.

_____
_____
_____
_____
_____
_____
_____

The cold, hard truth is that if we consider these verses to be applicable across all times, places, and people, then we cannot justify any participation in the abolition of slavery. The great Christian abolitionists were in the wrong. The participation of Christians in the Civil War was incredibly unjust. Furthermore, we should not be involved in any modern-day, anti-slavery mission; instead, we should be entreating slaves to respect and obey their masters "so that God's name and our teaching may not be slandered."

Read verses 2–3 again and circle Paul's warning about teaching anything other than what he is proposing in this letter. This is a pretty dire warning, isn't it? How, then, did we arrive at the place where we condemn slavery, almost universally, and actively fight against it?

Quite simply, someone, somewhere asked themselves: what is the intention here and what is the eternal word in this text? We're going to do the same together, right now. Answer the questions below.

What is the intention of these verses?

_____
_____
_____
_____

What is the eternal word, or timeless heart, of this text?

_____

_____

_____

Notice that elsewhere, in this same book, Paul lists "slave traders" as among a long list of ugly sins which are "contrary to the sound doctrine that conforms to the gospel" (1:10–11). What's more? Scripture (and Paul) widely condemns slavery (Exodus 21:16; Galatians 3:28; Colossians 4:1; Galatians 5:1) elsewhere. Therefore, it is only in allowing Scripture to interpret Scripture that we can justify taking the "heart" of what Paul is saying and leaving the literal outworking.

In modern America, we can ensure the keeping of the heart of this particular passage (keeping God's name from being slandered) by protecting human beings from slavery and defending the weak against exploitation. If we were to condone, and even make provisions for slavery, we would be bringing intense slander upon the name of God.

How does this principle apply to female subordination? Think of the ways God might be glorified by female subordination and list them below.

_____

_____

_____

_____

Now consider how female subordination might bring slander upon the name of the Lord. Write below what that might look like.

_____

_____

_____

If the timeless heart of these passages in 1 Timothy, which deal with women and slaves, is that God may be glorified in the world, consider how a modern-day adhering to a *words-on-page* application may undermine the very heart of what Paul was trying to accomplish. Our society, with the help of Christian ethics, is, thankfully, progressing beyond enslaving human beings and subordinating women. God's will of freedom for humankind is being done on earth as it is in heaven. If God's true notions are not being reflected in our modern-day applications of Scripture, and if a redemptive hermeneutic is not being used to apply the heart of Scripture while leaving behind ungodly cultural norms such as slavery and patriarchy, then we are failing to truly uphold a "high view" of Scripture.

What about Eve?

One of the main issues with 1 Timothy 2:12 is Paul's use of the word *authentein*, which is translated as "domineer" in the Latin Vulgate[5] and the New English Bible and as "usurp authority" in the King James Bible.

Authentein is used only once in Scripture. Paul usually used the word *exousia* when referring to authority in the church. Despite the debate surrounding Paul's choice of *authentein* in this passage, a few things are clear. This rare word packed a different punch than *exousia*. This wasn't teaching with authority that Paul was warning against; it was teaching with the intent to dominate.

Go back up to 1 Timothy 2:12–13 and circle the word for in verse 13. Some have argued that this word suggests a creation-order dictum. The word for in this verse is translated from the Greek word gar, which usually introduces an explanation for what comes next, not a cause (KJV Lexicon). If the meaning of verse 12 is that women are not to teach men in a domineering or controlling manner, then verse 13 explains why that is the case.

Read verse 13 and consider what Paul could mean by this verse. Then read verse 14 and consider what these verses mean together. Write your thoughts below.

_____

_____

_____

We've established previously that there is absolutely nothing in Scripture which indicates that the order of creation gave Adam any kind of inherent authority over Eve. Therefore, Paul cannot mean here that Adam being created first gives men across all time and all places immunity from the authoritative teachings of women. Linda Belleville posits that an interpretation which makes sense and flows with the other verses is that "Eve was created as Adam's partner and not his boss."

The Ephesians worshipped the goddess Artemis, and some theologians think that at least part of the false teaching Paul was addressing concerned runoff from the prevailing female-centric cult. This should inform our reading of the entirety of 1 Timothy, and especially of those verses pertaining to women. Paul's concern seems to be that women were attempting to dominate men in the assemblies, that they were flaunting social status, and that they were being led astray from taking care of their families and even from marrying at all. The point of verse 13, then, seems to be a reminder that Adam and Eve were partners.

---

[5] Latin Vulgate, Holy Bible Online

Verse 14 goes on to remind women that Eve was the one deceived, not Adam. Complementarians have used this verse to suggest that women are more prone to deception than men and, thus, unfit for authoritative teaching. However, a closer reading of the verse in context with the rest of the letter suggests that Paul was connecting Eve's deception as that of listening to the false teaching of the serpent, much like the false teachings that were apparently wreaking havoc in the Ephesian church.

Turn to 2 Corinthians 11:3 and record it below.

_____
_____
_____
_____
_____

Paul is addressing the entire congregation of the Corinthian church in this passage. What is his concern for them, men and women alike?

_____
_____
_____
_____
_____

Authentein

oth·en·teen

Greek Verb: To dominate, to usurp authority

Considering Paul's concern that every man, woman, and child in the Corinthian church could fall prey to a deception like Eve's and taking into account that every human heart is prone to deception (Jeremiah 17:9), describe your thoughts on whether or not women are more prone to deception and why.

_____
_____
_____
_____
_____
_____

Can you think of ways that the teaching that there is some sort of "deception" defect in every single female on earth could be seriously harmful to girls and women? Can you think of ways it could be harmful to the relationship between males and females (think mothers and sons, brothers and sisters, fathers and daughters, husbands and wives, bosses and employees, pastors and parishioners)? Relate your thoughts below.

_____
_____
_____
_____
_____
_____

In previous chapters, we've seen clearly in Scripture where women were active in the early churches, fully operating in the gifts of the Spirit, including prophesy, words of knowledge, teachings, and interpretations. We've proven, through the reading of Paul's other letters, that women were apostles, deacons, coworkers, and teachers as well. We've also established that the church in Ephesus was a unique body of believers, living in a particular time and place, who received a unique letter from Paul, instructing them on how to best live in the Greco-Roman culture of the time.

Taking all of this into account, what conclusions can you draw about why Paul is addressing the women of Ephesus in the manner found in verses 12–15?

_____
_____
_____
_____

Go back up and circle verse 15. A literal translation reads: "but women will be saved through *the* childbearing . . ." (emphasis mine). If these verses are a creation-order dictum, why is verse 15 not applied normatively? In other words, why do we not believe that child-bearing saves women? Give your insights below.

_____
_____
_____
_____
_____

Verse 15 cannot be understood without taking into account two important factors in Ephesian culture: 1) the previously mentioned widespread worship of Ephesian goddess Artemis (believed to be the protector of fertility) and the fact that many citizens of Ephesus were angry that, as Christianity spread, the money they made from this goddess worship was threatened (Acts 1).

2) the spreading of Gnosticism, a heretical movement sweeping through the 2nd century church which considered Eve (the spirit) to be superior to Adam (the soul) and taught, among many things, that celibacy was a way to master sexual powers that could eventually be used in a sort of "sexual priesthood." Abstinence was favored because the material world was rejected as evil.

While we do not know, exactly, the false teachings with which Paul was contending when he penned 1 Timothy, several verses give us clues that either of these factors, or perhaps a mixture of the two were influencing the early church in Ephesus. It's clear that Paul is concerned with women turning away from family life, marriage, and child bearing (5:9–15; 4:1–4), perhaps due to false teachings surrounding Artemis and/or Gnosticism which were circulating at that time.

If this is the case, then mystifying verse 15 becomes much clearer. Paul seems to be reminding the Ephesians that the physical act of child bearing is what brought about salvation for them (and the entire world) in *the* birth of Christ. The physical world, including marriage and family, is not to be despised or abandoned, for God is the One who created all of it.

This interpretation fits well with the Edenic reference when we recall God's curse to the serpent in Genesis. Write out Genesis 3:15 below.

_____
_____
_____

Does this interpretation make sense to you? Write your thoughts and any questions you might have.

_____
_____
_____

Can you think of any practical application for verse 15 in modern American society?

_____
_____
_____

Once again, we must ask ourselves the important questions.

What is the intention of verse 15?

_____
_____
_____

What is the timeless heart of this verse?

_____
_____
_____

Faith, love and holiness with propriety. These are God's true notions of what he wants for women and men alike.

The Ephesian women had their struggles, just as did their male contemporaries. The purpose of this study is to examine what Scripture has to say about female subordination, but we'd be remiss to ignore all that Scripture is saying to men as well. Very often, the heart of the verses used to clobber women into submission are restated elsewhere to men and women alike.

1 Timothy is a treasure trove of godly principles that can, and should, be valued by *all* Christians. This is discovered as we examine the timeless heart of what each passage is saying to us. Our task is to "accurately handle the word of truth" (2 Timothy 2:15) so that God's true notions are shining through every period in history and in the ages to come, in every geographical location, and to every culture and people group on earth. This task becomes impossible when we attempt half-baked cultural applications of Greco-Roman era social norms across all times, places, and people on earth.

We fail at upholding a high view of Scripture when we lose the heart of it along the way to application.

In the chapters to come, we will deal with more controversial passages and applications, but I hope we carry with us some of the valuable lessons 1 Timothy has taught us:

- Intention is everything.
- The lens of Christ is always necessary.
- Scripture interprets Scripture.
- The timeless heart is our ultimate goal.

Reflection & Discussion

1. It is interesting that many complementarian churches who don't permit women to teach, because of the belief that women are more prone to deception, *do* permit women to teach other women and children. Have you been in a church in which this was the case? Discuss how this subject was dealt with and how you felt about the chain of logic. Did you question it? Why or why not?

   _____
   _____
   _____
   _____
   _____

2. Discuss parallels between female subordination and slavery. Are there any differences? Any similarities? Can you reconcile the overthrowing of one and not the other? Why or why not?

   _____
   _____
   _____
   _____

3. Have you ever gotten the feeling that fear may be at the root of maintaining the "tortured hermeneutic" of gender hierarchy—fear of secular feminism, fear of losing wives and mothers, or fear of reverse subordination if women get "out of control?" Discuss how you think a lens of fear might affect our ability to accurately interpret the word of truth.

   _____
   _____
   _____
   _____
   _____

4. Another word for egalitarianism is mutuality. It's the idea that women and men were made for complete cooperation in God's kingdom and in the world. Discuss what this would look like if played out completely in the church. What would be the drawbacks? What would be the benefits?

   _____
   _____
   _____
   _____
   _____

5. Two notes of interest before we end the chapter: 1) The name of the apostle Junia has caused a long and controversial theological battle. The fact is that Junia is a female name and was changed by translators to Junias (the male form of the name). Despite the overwhelming evidence which demonstrates that Junia was both an apostle and a woman, many translations still do not reflect this truth. 2) In 1 Timothy 2:12, many translations include the word "must" (". . . she must be quiet"). However, a literal Greek rendering does not include the word must at all. This word has literally been added by translators. Moreover, the literal Greek reads like this: "but to be in quietness (or stillness)." The idea is more like "gentleness," according to many theologians. Discuss why you think these words have been changed by translators. List as many possibilities as you can. How does this affect the way you view these passages?

   _____
   _____
   _____
   _____
   _____
   _____

Lyla's Story

By this age, Lyla thought she'd be married with children. She hadn't set out to live the life of a single Christian, which could be a lonely life indeed.

Eagerly—perhaps too eagerly at times—she'd attended singles' events at church, mixed and mingled wherever she could, and even joined an online Christian dating service. Yet, here she was, thirty-seven and with no husband or children to show for her efforts.

Recently, she'd hit what she believed to be a crisis point. She'd purposely held herself back from advancing in her career at the bank where she worked because she didn't want to be distracted if the opportunity for marriage presented itself. More importantly, she didn't want to appear to be a career-obsessed man-eater if Mr. Right did come along.

As a single woman, she'd found that she was limited in ministry as well. Of course, children's church and Sunday school classes were always available options, so she dutifully showed up week after week, faithful to an area of ministry to which she neither felt called or spiritually gifted to do.

When she took an honest evaluation of her life, she became downright depressed. She loved her job at the bank but definitely felt she'd hit a plateau. She regretted passing by several offers of advancement throughout the years. Her boss once confronted her, saying, "Lyla, you're obviously a leader, and we could really use your expertise in upper management. What's the problem?"

Her response now seemed pathetic in retrospect: "Sir, I appreciate your confidence in me; but I think I have enough on my plate right now."

The truth was that she didn't have nearly enough on her plate. She'd been foolishly waiting for Mr. Right to show up so that her life could finally begin. Every day of her adult life had been nothing more than going through the motions. Most of the people in her church didn't know what to say to her anymore. After she hit thirty, and with no prospects for marriage on the horizon, she began to see a pity in her friends' eyes that made her sick on the inside.

Her boss was right—she was a natural leader. She had a knack for seeing the big picture, implementing plans to correct problems, and harnessing the gifts and talents of those around her for the greater good. At work and in the children's ministry, she was the one people turned to for mentorship.

Yet, she'd never truly thrown herself into a passion project. She'd never even allowed herself to have a passion, beyond building a healthy marriage and family. Her mother, her aunts, and all the women she'd admired in church growing up reminded her continually that this was her purpose.

Women were created to be helpmeets. That was her mother's mantra.

That mantra, meant to be a guiding light for her, had turned into shackles for her soul. What was she supposed to do with that statement? She'd done all that she could to make herself attractive and had prepared to be a wife and mother. She'd thrown herself into her so-called purpose.

Yet all she had to show for it was a half-baked career, unfulfilling ministry, stagnant spiritual giftings, and a thoroughly exhausted spirit.
If she wasn't going to be married and had indeed been called to a life of singleness, where was her place as a woman in the body of Christ? Where was her place in the world?

She longed to pour her passion and her entire being into something that would have everlasting significance in the eyes of Jesus. If a family wasn't going to be that *something*, what was? What was she to do with these obvious leadership gifts? Let them lie dormant? Were her talents to be buried?

These questions burned in her heart. If she'd failed in some way, she wished God would show her. For the first time in her life, she began to wonder if he even cared at all.

Headship and Head Coverings

Despite the fact that the overwhelming majority of evangelical Christians believe that any human mediator between God and the Christian is unnecessary, this foundational principle of the faith is often pushed to the side when it comes to females in the church. Often, the husband is exalted as the "spiritual head" of the household and the pastors and elders as the spiritual "authority" of the church. Women, it is believed by complementarians, are to operate under the covering of headship both at home and in church. Thus, a woman's father is often seen as her spiritual authority until she is wed; at which time, the spiritual headship baton is passed to her husband. Ultimately, females in the church may fall under the umbrella of several layers of headship as time goes on—father, husband, male pastor, male elders, male Bible study teachers, and male leaders in the congregation.

This is an important point because, as is often the case when spiritual authority and headship are taught and practiced from the complementarian viewpoint, it's conceivable that females may never have any real say-so over their spiritual headship. Certainly, a daughter cannot consent to the father to whom she's born. Though she has agency in who she chooses as a mate, her spiritual autonomy is severely limited after the wedding day. Therefore, she must submit to her husband's decisions on where they worship and, thus, who her spiritual leadership is within the church. Of course, many complementarian husbands listen to and respond to the feelings and opinions of their wives in all matters, but especially in matters of worship. However, when push comes to shove, the ultimate decision lies with the spiritual head of the household. Obviously, this puts females in the position of possibly never having complete agency in many matters of religious devotion and practice.

The stakes are set high, aren't they? We're talking about lives spent living by these doctrines, marriages operating under these imperatives, families built on these foundations, churches full with half of their members exercising spiritual authority over the other half.

With so much on the line, it's of the utmost importance to understand what Scripture has to say about headship and spiritual authority, especially in regard to female subordination.

So, what is spiritual authority and who has it? Under what circumstances is it given and taken away and by whom? What does spiritual authority entail and what are its limits? When it is in practice, and what does it look like?

These questions are at the heart of the ongoing debate surrounding patriarchy and female subordination. This chapter dives right in to understanding the nature of spiritual authority according to Scripture. As always, we bring our findings from the previous studies as well as the lens of Christ through which we must view all things if we want to arrive at truth.

Let's begin by turning in our Bibles to 1 Corinthians 11:2–16 because this large swath of Scripture is used most often to silence women in churches and to keep them in submission at home. Unfortunately, this passage is often cited as one of the "clear cut" places where Scripture prescribes female subordination. I use the word *unfortunate* because, as we will see, this passage is *anything* but clear. Indeed, this portion of Scripture is regarded by many scholars as one of the most confusing in all of the Bible. Therefore, we will give it our full attention and proceed thoroughly through each verse, trying to find God's true notions as we go.

Write out verses 2–6 in the space below.

_____
_____
_____
_____
_____
_____
_____

Now, go back up and circle every instance of the word "head" found in the verses above. The Greek word for head used here is *kephale*. Much debate, speculation, and outright squabbling has been centered around this one word. At first blush, it seems rather cut-and-dried: go to the Greek lexicon, find the original meaning, and then stick it in the verse and move on.

Yet, this simple method becomes problematic because the word in question has several distinct meanings in the original Greek. *Kephale* is one of those words that is found throughout Greek literature and has a variety of usages. Therefore, scholars must scour and record every instance of the word and its possible meanings. These findings must be compiled and then they have to be painstakingly applied to the Scripture or piece of literature at hand. As you can imagine, this leaves a lot of room for debate as to which meaning should be used in a particular verse. To add further difficulty, the possible meanings continue to expand as ancient literature is discovered and words studied.

This point cannot be emphasized enough—there is no "plain reading" of 1 Corinthians 11:2–16 because: 1) of the way Paul worded this passage; 2) the highly debated meaning of *kephale*, upon which the entirety of the passages hinges; and 3) the culture to which Paul is writing. However, too much is at stake to skim over it and refuse to dig deep because of the difficulties of interpretation. This passage is used to cut at the heart of female equality—dredging up the creation order debate and calling into question a woman's ability to exercise authority over her own life and soul.

So, what are the possible meanings of the word *kephale*? In the Old Testament, the Hebrew word *rosh*, sometimes translated *kephale* in Greek, is used hundreds of times as literally describing the head on a body or top of a tower or mountain. However, there are over 180 uses of the word *rosh* in the Old Testament as a metaphor for leader or chieftain, and, in these instances, the word *rosh* is translated as *arche* ("leader").[6] An important thing to keep in mind here is that the Old Testament Hebrew is not as applicable to this argument as many would like to imagine. Considering Paul was writing this letter to a Roman/Greek audience, they would have had no understanding of the Hebrew word rosh as their Greek Bibles would have already had the words translated. Yet, because many complementarians reach back to the Old Testament as evidence that *kephale* means "authority," these translations must be understood.

Do you find any significance in the use of the word *rosh* in the Old Testament as evidence for the meaning of *kephale* as found in 1 Corinthians 11? Describe why or why not below.

_____

_____

_____

Kephale

kef·al·ay'

Greek Lexicon: Noun: head; alternatively, source or grounding of one's being

The word kephale in Greek literally means "head," and many of its extrabiblical uses reflect this literal meaning. Some other meanings are "beginning or source," "prominent or preeminent part," "source of the body's working systems," "ground of being," and "sum," to name a few possibilities that seem to fit with the reading of the passage at hand. However, one word that kephale never means, in any extrabiblical source, is "authority." [7] Paul uses the Greek word archon ("leader") in Romans 13:3, and he uses the word exousia ("authority") many times in 1 Corinthians and Romans. The word kephale, however, cannot be translated directly as "authority." Authority, as a possible meaning of kephale, can be rightly discussed and debated, but it cannot be rightly assumed and automatically inserted. Therefore, any reading of 1 Corinthians (or any other passage), which substitutes "authority" in place of "head," is erroneous and any application of this passage with that substitution in mind is flat wrong.

Our task then, as students of the Word of God, as seekers of God's true notions, is to find the meaning that most makes sense in the metaphor Paul is employing. Paul uses *kephale* in three ways elsewhere in his writings:

1. to describe Christ's relationship to the church (Ephesians 4:15–16, 5:23; Colossians 1:18, 2:19);
2. to describe Christ's relationship to the "powers" (Ephesians 1:22; Colossians 2:10); and
3. to describe a householder's relationship to his wife (Ephesians 5:23).

Record Ephesians 4:15–16 below:

_____
_____
_____
_____
_____
_____

This passage is describing Christ's relationship to the church. List a few words that describe the sort of relationship that our *kephale* has to us as described in this passage written by the same Paul who wrote 1 Corinthians.

_____
_____
_____
_____
_____

---

[7] Swanson, J. Dictionary of Biblical Languages with Semantic Domains: Greek (New Testament) (electronic ed.) (Oak Harbor: Logos Research Systems, Inc., 1997).

Now go back to some of the possible meanings of kephale listed above and write down which ones you find most fitting to Ephesians 4:15–16.

_____
_____
_____

Do any not seem to fit? Why or why not?

_____
_____
_____

Let's look at Colossians 2:19 and record it below.

_____
_____
_____
_____

Once again, review the possible meanings of kephale and write down which ones you find to be most fitting to Colossians 2:19.

_____
_____
_____

Do any of the meanings not fit? Why or why not?

_____
_____
_____

Are there any hints of authority or submission, of subjugation or superiority hinted at in the Ephesians or the Colossians passages? Alternatively, do these passages seem to suggest a life-giving, supportive source of supply for the body's natural processes? Consider these two very different meanings of this one word carefully. Write your thoughts below.

_____
_____
_____

Read back over 1 Corinthians 11:2–6 again. Insert some of the different meanings of kephale into those verses. Pray over these different readings. Consider the totality of Scripture we have uncovered so far. Make sure you have the lens of Christ on your spiritual eyes as you look at these verses again and again. Commentators can only offer you their own opinions of the meaning of this metaphor. Lexicons and dictionaries can only offer you the possibilities of what these words can mean. Ultimately, it is up to you and the Holy Spirit to rightly divide the Word of Truth here. I can't do it for you, and no one else should be able to either.

Which meaning makes the most sense to you and why? Take time answering this question before moving on. This is of the utmost importance in your journey.

_____
_____
_____
_____
_____
_____
_____
_____

What is Paul's primary concern in these verses?

_____
_____

An important point must be made about the words "the head of Christ is God" in verse 3 because this verse has been used by some to signify that Christ is eternally subordinate to Father God. Indeed, proponents of female subordination (on the basis of this passage) are forced into this conclusion by their own logic. However, ample evidence in Scripture points to the fact that Jesus is Lord (Romans 10:9), he is God (Hebrews 1:8; Romans 9:5; John 1:1), and that not only is he equal with God (Philippians 2:6), but his subordination was limited (Philippians 2:7). Paul calls Christ "head over everything" and Revelation 22:1 and 3 paints a picture of Jesus (the Lamb) ruling with God on the throne forever.

What is your understanding of the relationship within the Trinity?

_____
_____
_____

Once again, taking into consideration the totality of Scripture, it's a grave error to impose an artificial hierarchical relationship into the Trinity. This understanding of the Trinity breaks with orthodoxy and Scripture and, therefore, must be rejected.

How does your understanding of the pairs mentioned in the passage (Christ-man, woman-man, and Christ-God) change if you remove the notion of hierarchy?

_____
_____
_____
_____

Theologian Kevin Jiles condemns the idea of eternal subordination of Christ to God and of woman to man on the basis that these relationships are being defined in terms of the broken human relations resulting from the fall, where "some rule and others obey and where people are differentiated according to the authority they exercise or are excluded from exercising."[8]

Envision human relationships operating in mutuality and harmony as does the Trinity. What does this look like to you?

_____
_____
_____
_____

Now let's move forward and look at the rest of our primary passage in 1 Corinthians. Record verses 7–12 below.

_____
_____
_____
_____
_____
_____
_____

So far, the head/body relationship hasn't been established in 1 Corinthians, but the "ground of the other's being" option of the word kephale seems to be firmly laid out in

---

[8] Giles, Kevin. The Trinity and Subordinationism: The Doctrine of God and the Contemporary Gender Debate (Downers Grove, Ill: Intervarsity Press, 2002).

11:8 and 11:12. Insert this meaning into these two verses and see if they make sense to you as well. Write your observations below.

_____

Verse 7 talks about man being the "image and the glory of God" and woman being the "glory of man." What does this suggest to you in terms of what the woman brings to the man?

_____

What we can gather for certain from 1 Corinthians 11 is that Paul was intensely concerned with honor and shame in the cultural setting of the Corinthian church. He warned men not to bring dishonor on God through their outward actions (covering their heads) and, likewise, he warned women not to bring dishonor on the men through their outward actions (not covering their heads). Paul uses the terms: "shame," "fitting/proper," "nature," and "custom" to convey this idea.

There is widespread agreement among theologians that head coverings (and lack thereof) were apparently important in the Corinthian culture in terms of honor and shame; therefore, Paul is concerned that women and men bring honor to God and to one another through their outward actions and appearances. However, there is also widespread agreement that, since head coverings have no cultural significance in the modern Western world, these imperatives are able to be set aside as obsolete. Rather, we search for the timeless truth, God's true notions, in this passage.

As previously explored in other chapters, the timeless truth here is that we are to behave in culturally honorable ways, despite our freedoms in Christ, in order to bring glory to God.

Describe some outward signs of honor that translate into our current culture.

_____

Verses 8–9 seem to be explaining how the woman is, indeed, the glory of man. Complementarians point to these verses as evidence that women were created for the express purpose of bringing something (glory, honor, help, companionship, etc.) to men but not vice versa. Once again, hierarchy has to be imposed onto this passage in order to arrive at the conclusion that God created females to be subordinate to males. I defer to the prominent theologian, Gordon Fee, for a simple understanding of these verses. He notes that Paul is alluding to the Old Testament text of creation in these verses and that he's emphasizing the *incompleteness* of man by himself.

"The animals will not do; he needs one who is bone of his bone, one who is like him but different from him, one who is uniquely his own 'glory.' In fact, when the man in the Old Testament narrative sees the woman, he 'glories' in her by bursting into song."[9]

How can we be sure that Paul was not teaching, as complementarians propose, that these verses plainly suggest female subordination as imposed by creation order? The answer is very simply because of verses 11–12. Too often, these beautiful, powerful verses are overlooked. Read through them again, slowly. Take in the beautiful picture that is being painted here. We, as men and women, are not independent of one another. We both come from each other and from God. Fee summarizes how these verses help to explain the preceding ones: "She is not thereby subordinate to him but necessary for him. She exists to his honor as the one who having come from man is the one companion suitable to him, so that he might be complete and that together they might form humanity."

Pause to consider whether, head coverings aside, Paul is describing a hierarchical relationship here or one of mutuality. Read also 1 Corinthians 7:1–5. What are God's true intentions for the nature of the man-woman relationship, according to these verses? Record your thoughts below.

---

[9] Fee, Gordon. First Epistle to the Corinthians, Revised Edition (Eerdmans, 2014), 571.

Let's now turn to verse 10. The word translated as "authority" in NIV is the Greek word *exousia*, which literally means "authority/right to act." This is an extremely unexpected word choice because if Paul meant subjection (as complementarians assert), then why does he employ a word that means "authority/right to act"? Many translators have taken care of this problem by translating the word *exousia* to mean "veil" and "sign of authority." Unfortunately for proponents of these translations, Paul uses *exousia* extensively in 1 Corinthians and, each time, the direct meaning is "authority/right to act."

We need to pause here and consider why translators would substitute "veil" or "sign of authority" in place of the obvious meaning of *exousia* in all of 1 Corinthians—"authority/right to act." Once again, we're face-to-face with what can happen when people—even biblical scholars—come into contact with theology that doesn't fit inside the box they've created to understand the complexities of the relationship between God-man-woman-Christ-church. Just as egalitarians must deal head-on with the passages of Scripture that make them uncomfortable, complementarians must do the same.

We are only hurting ourselves, as the body of Christ, by ignoring, altering, or side-stepping the complex, nuanced, mysterious notions of God as outlined in Scripture.

Write down your thoughts on the difference an understanding of the meaning of this one word—*exousia*—makes in understanding the nature of authority in male-female relationships. Consider what is at stake when words like this are altered on purpose to advance a particular interpretation.

Exousia

ex·oo·see·ah

Greek Lexicon: Noun; Power of choice, liberty as doing as one pleases, physical or mental power, power of authority

The phrase "because of the angels" in verse 10 continues to be mystifying to most theologians. Many theories have been presented, including the following (most plausible):

- Angelos, the Greek word translated "angel" here is actually better translated "messengers." This could mean that messengers were being sent from various groups to check out the new Christian communities and see what they were about. If this is the case, Paul would have been concerned that the Corinthian Christians, in breaking with the cultural traditions of the people around them, were bringing dishonor to one another and to God through their actions. A reading of verse 10, which has this in mind, is: "It is for this reason that a woman ought to have authority/the right to act over her own head, because of the messengers." In other words, a woman ought to use the authority she has over own head wisely so as to bring honor to God, herself, and others. This understanding falls in line with Paul's previous usage of exousia as found in 1 Corinthians 8:9 and 9:1–23, in which he admonishes faulty employment of personal authority.

- A compelling argument is that the Corinthian Christians were apparently obsessed with angels and angelic language (speaking in tongues) and were overemphasizing angels/angelic ways of being in their congregation. Paul mentions angels several times in 1 Corinthians (4:9; 6:2–3; 13:1). According to Gordon Fee, this view of a higher spirituality could account for "some women's (apparent) rejection of the marriage bed (1 Corinthians 7:1–7; because they are already as the angels), so much so that they could even argue for divorce if need be (1 Corinthians 7:10–16). It also accounts for their (possibly) discouraging some "virgins" already promised in marriage from following through (1 Corinthians 7:25–38) and for some men's resorting to prostitutes as a result (1 Corinthians 6:12–20)."[10] He goes on to note that this could also account for their emphasis on "words of knowledge," "wisdom," and the casting off of physical gender distinctions in the matter of hair. If this is the case, the verse would mean something like this: "If you're worried about the angels, consider the dishonor you're bringing on your own head, the head of your husband, and God by behaving in a way that is seen as shameful to those around you."

---

[10] Fee, Gordon. Praying and Prophesying in the Assemblies: 1 Corinthians 11:2-16. (Discovering Biblical Equality: Complementarity without Hierarchy). Downers Grove, IL, Intervarsity Press, 2005.

Do either of these interpretations ring true to you? Write your thoughts on this highly debated verse below.

_____

_____

_____

_____

_____

In the end, Paul concludes with a challenge to the Corinthians to judge for themselves what is proper (v. 13), and he appeals to nature itself as well as to the accepted practice of the churches of God. Realizing that some would be contentious on this issue, he left the matter with this forceful persuasion.

This question bears repeated asking: If Paul is making such a forceful persuasion as to the glory of woman being her long hair and the disgrace of man the cutting of his, why do we not adhere to these standards in the modern age?

Simply put, we understand that these things are no longer disgraceful and/or honorable in our current culture.

I lived in a Muslim country for several years, and one of the standards we chose to live by as respectful expatriates was to wear conservative clothing. This meant that I didn't don a bikini to go to the pool or wear a low-cut blouse on a date with my husband. This meant that I covered even my shoulders when out in public and wore cropped pants instead of shorts, no matter how hot it was outside. These were things I did as a sign of respect for the culture in which I lived.

In America, our cultural standards are completely different. Some folks are more conservative than others, but it's generally not dishonorable to see women wearing shorts, bikinis, earrings, or short hairstyles. The average American would not visit a church, see women in make-up, short hair, and dressed nicely and decide, then and there, to avoid Christianity because the folks who call themselves Christians are dishonoring to the culture.

However, non-churched people have reported, time and again, about the judgment they felt concerning outward appearances coming *from* the church. Likewise, the unchurched loudly report feeling uncomfortable, even horrified, with the church's stance on the subordination of females. Instead of considering how best to behave in an honorable fashion in our current age and culture, many Christians are almost militant in hanging on to outdated customs for the sole purpose of being countercultural!

Have you ever visited or lived in another culture? Describe your experience and whether or not you had to make any concessions in order to show honor to a culture very different from your own.

_____
_____
_____
_____
_____

Now that we've surveyed 1 Corinthians 11, let's consider what is at the timeless heart of these verses. Instead of me giving you my opinion here, I'd like for you to review all that has been laid out above and also your answers to the prompts. Pray about this question and answer honestly. What is the timeless heart of this passage?

_____
_____
_____
_____
_____

As we move into the next chapter on spiritual giftings, I hope you'll take with you some of the principles we've established so far.

- God created males and females equally, perfectly, and for the purpose of mutual companionship and work on the earth.

- Sin is the corrupter of God's perfect design.

- Jesus came to bring God's Kingdom to earth as it is in heaven. In Him, we are all joint heirs and the equal in access to God and to all of the gifts of the Holy Spirit.

- Whatever headship might mean, it is clear that the ultimate goal of every Christian is to exercise humility, love, honor and servanthood in relationships.

- If we apply a portion of Scripture literally, we must consider and defend why we do not apply the entirety of Scripture literally.

- Our current age and culture are drastically different than the Greco-Roman culture in which Paul lived and from which perspective he wrote; therefore, there will be culturally specific imperatives that no longer translate into our culture and time. It's our task to discern when an adjustment is required, while always staying true to the timeless heart, or God's true notions, in Scripture.

Reflection & Discussion

1. Discuss your understanding of headship and how this is played out in the churches, marriages, and Christian circles of which you've been a part.

2. What are the equivalent of "head coverings" that may bring shame or honor in our age and time?
   _____
   _____
   _____

3. Which of the points in this chapter resonated with you the most? Which caused you to object?
   _____
   _____
   _____

4. Think about the healthiest marriages you've ever witnessed. Now think about the most dysfunctional. Discuss the qualities you've observed in both.

5. Consider the ramifications of raising young girls in the church. On the one hand, there's an obvious need to prepare girls to live successfully in an egalitarian world, and, moreover, there's an obvious need to teach them how to exercise agency in their personal faith journeys. On the other hand, young girls are being taught that they were created to be helpmeets to men, that they must always operate under male spiritual authority, and that, ultimately, the male headship in their lives will always supersede their own autonomy, at least on some level. What issues could arise from this double message? Have you seen any second or third term effects come from these conflicting worldviews?
   _____
   _____
   _____
   _____
   _____

Spiritual Gifts and Agency

From pretty early on, one can usually detect the natural gifts and talents of a person. One child may display a keen mind for mechanics and another an aptitude for cooking. One may be fixated on the sciences while another may always be found spear-heading games and competitions in the neighborhood.

We all come installed with some natural gifts and talents and often pick up a few more as life goes along.

Likewise, when a person becomes saved in Christ, spiritual gifts are given from God. A Holy Spirit installation begins as soon as God breathes His new life into us. Both men and women alike will receive power from on high to accomplish certain tasks and reveal a little of God's character to the world through the use of these gifts.

Both complementarians and egalitarians agree that all God's children receive spiritual giftings. However, disagreement arises as to who can receive particular spiritual gifts and in what context they are able to exercise them. This chapter will tackle the big question of whether or not the Holy Spirit differentiates between gender when it comes to spiritual gifting.

Before we jump into the Scripture, perhaps a little reflection is in order. What is your understanding of the "prerequisites" for being gifted by the Holy Spirit?

_____
_____
_____
_____

What do you feel are your spiritual gifts? Have you ever received confirmation from others in these gifts? Share below.

_____
_____
_____

What are your natural talents and abilities? Do they differ from the spiritual gifts you mentioned above?

_____
_____
_____

What are the "good spiritual works" God has done through you, specifically using your natural talents and your spiritual giftings?

_____
_____
_____
_____

Turn to Ephesians 2:10 and record it below.

_____
_____
_____
_____

This verse describes us as God's handiwork and states clearly that we have preordained jobs to do, for which we have been prepared in advance. Spiritual gifts are, therefore, different than our natural talents. Though our natural talents may certainly be used in ministry, spiritual giftings are specially designed and bestowed for the good spiritual works God gives us to accomplish.

Let's turn back to 1 Corinthians and record 12:7 below.

_____
_____
_____
_____

Circle the words "manifestation of the Spirit" in the verse written above. This powerful verse demonstrates unequivocally that each and every believer—simply because they are a member of the body of Christ—receives a manifestation of the Spirit for the common good.

There's no prerequisite, and there's no differentiation between each believer. Each one manifests the Holy Spirit for the common good of all. There's no limit on who will receive the benefits of the manifested Spirit in each person's life. In other words, I may be edified, taught, corrected, and encouraged by the Holy Spirit manifested in a small child just as well as I may benefit in all of those ways from the Holy Spirit manifested in a prominent theologian. I may benefit from the Holy Spirit in a woman just as well as I may benefit from the Holy Spirit in a man. It's not about the vessel, but it's about the Spirit poured into and out of the vessel.

Let's also record 1 Corinthians 12:11 in the space below.

_____
_____
_____

Go back up and circle the words "as He wills." This is important because, often, we take it upon ourselves to limit who can receive what spiritual gift, despite the fact that we have zero control in this area. The Scripture here is clear—the Holy Spirit distributes the giftings according to His will. The bottom line, according to this verse is that our opinions, judgments, ideas, and even our theological beliefs do not determine who receives what particular spiritual gifts.

Have you ever made a judgment on someone's spiritual gifts? What criteria did you use to judge?

_____
_____
_____
_____

Since we've established that it is the Holy Spirit's job and authority to determine which spiritual gifts each and every believer will receive, the question becomes simple: does the Holy Spirit require maleness as the first step in receiving the particular gifts of leadership, preaching, and teaching?

If it's God's true notion that males are outfitted for leadership roles in the church and that females are not, surely Scripture will be crystal clear on this matter, right?

In order to determine what roles from which women are excluded, we must first examine the roles in question. What does the Bible say about leadership roles, church office, and structure? Many complementarians begin with the Old Testament, reaching back to the establishment of the Jewish priesthood. The argument here is that because only men were allowed to be priests in ancient Israel, this is God's understood stamp of approval on male-only leadership in church structure.

Laying aside the obvious problems of overlaying Old Testament law on top of the New Covenant Church as well as dragging in ancient culture and tradition into modern-day family and church structure, complementarians still fall short on this argument simply because they are up against Old and New Testament Scripture on this matter.

Turn to Exodus 19:6 and record it below.

_____
_____
_____

Turn to Isaiah 61:6 and record it below.

_____
_____
_____

God established a male priesthood in Israel. This is undeniable, though why he chose males can be debated. However, what matters here is His ultimate goal, His true notions, and the timeless heart of this loving God. The two Scriptures above make it crystal clear what the heart of God is on this matter. Below, describe what you infer from the Exodus and Isaiah passages above.

_____
_____
_____
_____

Turn to 1 Timothy 2:5 and describe below who is now the one mediator between mankind and God.

_____
_____
_____

Read Hebrews 7:11–28 and record your observations about the extent of Jesus's priesthood. Why was the Old Testament priesthood not sufficient? How is Jesus the only priest we will ever need?

_____
_____
_____
_____

Week 8: Spiritual Gifts and Agency

When we set up spiritual hierarchy in our homes and churches, we run the risk of elevating human beings above Jesus Christ and the reality of the Holy Spirit in our lives. Complementarians paint a picture of loving husbands, fathers, pastors, elders, and teachers serving as "priests of the home" or "shepherds of the flock" without taking into consideration how this paradigm undermines the very work and role of Christ, both in the lives of males and females.

Can you think of any ways that males can be harmed by the understanding that they somehow serve as priests to women but not vice versa? Describe what you've seen or what you can imagine it would be like to live with the burden of "standing in" for Christ both at home and at church but with no reciprocation?

_____
_____
_____
_____
_____
_____

In light of the biblical evidence which demonstrates that the Levitical priesthood is a past structure, established for a particular period of time, for a particular purpose which has now reached ultimate fulfillment in Christ, what priestly roles do believers still have in the world and to one another?

Turn to Galatians 3:26–28 and record it below.

_____
_____
_____
_____
_____

Why do you think Paul would include male and female in a list of the social and religious hierarchy that Christ abolished? Stop and honestly consider this point. Give your thoughts below.

_____
_____
_____
_____

Paul doesn't offer any exceptions here. For example, he doesn't say: You're are all one in Christ, there is no more hierarchy at all—except for when it comes to females and males. Females have always been, and will always be, subordinate to males. This is the way God wants it and has designed it, even in light of what Christ has accomplished for all of mankind.

Let's pause here and consider together why this passage (and all of Galatians) is so important to our Christian theology. Paul is essentially saying that the old way of categorizing people— according to ethnicity, gender, and social status (hierarchical relationships)—is over. In Christ, we are now one. A thorough treatment of Galatians is beyond the scope of this study, but it would be beneficial to read the book in its entirety because Paul talks of a new order established in Christ, one where value is no longer assigned to ethnicity, gender, and status. As Gordon Fee so aptly puts it: "The Jewish free woman is now 'Christ's slave;' the Gentile male slave is 'Christ's freedman' (1 Corinthians 7:19–24). The sociological categories count for nothing; how one lives within the categories count for everything."[11]

Therefore, this passage in Galatians must be completely ignored if we are to maintain a hierarchical viewpoint regarding males and females in the church. Not only that, but we must put aside the "oneness in Christ" Paul talks about in the text. Furthermore, we must embrace the cultural norms of a fallen world rather than embracing the new thing that has been accomplished in Christ.

Let's turn to another passage, more directly dealing with biblical priesthood. Read 1 Peter 2:9 and record it below.

_____

_____

_____

Circle the word "declare" in the verse above. Some synonyms of declare are: proclaim, announce, state, reveal, articulate, publicize, and broadcast. According to this verse, we are all part of a priesthood of believers in Christ, tasked with the purpose of declaring the praises of God.

This verse establishes two things: 1.) Females are indeed members of the royal priesthood of believers, every bit as equal and equipped as their brothers; and 2.) Females are tasked with verbal ministry every bit as much as their brothers in Christ.

Once again, we find no evidence of females receiving "less of" or "differently functioning" gifts of the Holy Spirit. In fact, we find just the opposite. What's incredibly interesting is that there are no intentional instructions as to women performing in leadership roles in

---

[11] Fee, Gordon. 2005). Male and Female in the New Creation. Discovering Biblical Equality: Complementarity without Hierarchy. Intervarsity Press: Downers Grove, IL.

the church, either for or against. 1 Timothy 3:1–13 and Titus 1:5–9 outline qualifications for certain positions in the church. Take a moment to read those passages of Scripture and jot down your observations below.

_____

_____

_____

_____

_____

_____

_____

Take a look back at 1 Timothy 3:11 because this passage is very important. The NIV contains the following footnote for this verse: "Possibly deacon's wives or women who are deacons." If one reads 1 Timothy, chapter 3 in its totality, without bringing any presuppositions to the table, verse 11 stands out clearly as specific instructions to women who are deacons. This is no surprise when we remember that Paul called Phoebe a deacon (Romans 6:1–2). So, though there are many requisites for elders, overseers, and deacons in the church, being male is not one of them according to this passage, as well as others.

The Titus passage, however, is directed toward men only. Complementarians often cite this portion of Scripture as evidence that only males are gifted to be leaders in the church. The argument goes: If women were to be included in leadership positions, wouldn't this passage address them as well?

At first glance, this point seems valid. There's no mention of women's qualifications for leadership positions in this text. However, the absence of a prescriptive does not a new prescriptive make! Paul's approach to women in leadership, as we've already established, is different according to the circumstance and people group (Philippians 4:23; 1 Corinthians 11:5; Romans 16:1–2). To draw the conclusion that women cannot be elders, deacons, teachers, or preachers simply because Paul offered guidance for male leaders in one portion of Scripture is more than a stretch, especially in light of all he wrote about women elsewhere.

We've established in previous chapters that women did, indeed, participate in all activities of ministry (Acts 18:26; 1 Corinthians 14:26, 29–31). We've also established that the gifts of the Spirit are administered according to His will and not on a basis of gender or any other form of status.

> **Furthermore, we've established that women are created equally to men and that there is no biblical evidence for any sort of deficiency within them based upon their femaleness.**

We've also established that there is no explicit instruction as to women's roles in leadership. There may be implications found in particular passages, such as the Titus Scripture noted above, but there are valid counterarguments available from other portions of Scripture as well.

Consider the Lord's Supper. We are offered only implied teachings in this area and nothing explicit. There is no step-by-step guide for how to conduct the Lord's Supper, who is meant to perform what task, where and when to initiate it, etc. Therefore, the diverse readings of the texts have led to an array of traditions within the church. Every denomination believes that they have the "right" way to administer the Lord's Supper, and yet they all base their beliefs upon the same passages of Scripture. This is a great example of how different interpretations of implied prescriptives may yield different results.

On the flip side, certain *explicit* prescriptives, such as found in 1 Corinthians 14:39 in which Paul states, "Therefore, my brothers and sisters, be eager to prophesy and do not forbid speaking in tongues," are ignored because of culture. When is the last time you walked into church and were met with folks all over who were eager to prophesy? What about speaking in tongues? This is a directive given from Paul that is pushed to the wayside because this sort of activity in most modern-day, American churches is not normal.

> **The stakes are too high in the female subordination debate to be wishy-washy theologically or to cherry pick which prescriptives to follow and which to ignore.**

This cannot be overemphasized—entire families, marriages, churches, and para-church organizations are affected by the doctrine that females are subordinate to males across all time and cultures.

By now, we've surveyed a large swath of Paul's teachings regarding females in the church, as well as his teachings regarding spirit giftedness and the new thing God has created in Christ. If you're like me, you've wondered how Paul can say one thing to the Corinthians (and even that can vary from chapter to chapter), then another thing to the Romans, and yet another thing to the Galatians. What's the deal? Either women can be deacons and fellow apostles, or they must be silent, submissive learners. Why does Paul seem to flip-flop on this issue?

The book of Galatians may hold the answer to that question. Reread the Galatians passage you recorded above. If you have time, read the entire letter. A theme that seems to come to the forefront is this new thing God is doing through Christ. He has, and is, upturning our old, fallen human structures (gender, social status, religious superiority) and has leveled the entire playing field. This notion was radical—those who previously served you are now the ones you serve, as a Christian! However, Paul is completely disinterested in establishing some new world order. He understands and imparts to us that this New Kingdom is inside of us and, as the body of Christ, it's in between us. Therefore, when he cautions the Corinthians to behave in a way that brings honor to Christ amongst their pagan neighbors, he is not condoning any sort of social and cultural system of patriarchy. He is simply saying: these structures no longer matter to us because of the new thing God is doing. *They only have value insofar as they can help you bear witness to the glory of God among your neighbors.*

There is no longer slave nor free, Jew nor Greek, male nor female. We are all, radically and gloriously, one in Christ. It stands to reason that, as God's holy church, we should be moving toward this true notion of God and not away. If we lived in a patriarchal culture, we would take great care to follow the wise instructions of Paul to limit our freedoms (for a time) for the sake of bringing honor to God. However, we don't live in that sort of culture in modern America. The culture, sadly, is outpacing the church in heralding equality for females. Once again, we must examine what kind of witness we're sending to the world.

Let's do a check-in. What are your thoughts regarding God's true notions about spirit-giftedness, gender, and leadership roles at this point? Provide details below.

_____
_____
_____
_____
_____

Many complementarians, in light of the preponderance of evidence, finally agree that women can be gifted to teach and even preach, they can even hold positions of leadership, but with one caveat—they can only teach, preach to, and lead *other women*. Though Scripture itself does not establish this rule, many churches implement it, nonetheless.

Have you ever been a part of a church, Bible study, or other organization that allowed women to teach and preach to other women but not to men? What did this look like, practically speaking?

_____
_____

Situations like this beg the question: If a woman is qualified and gifted to teach/preach to an audience of females, why is she not qualified to teach males? If her message is true, biblical, and God-honoring, how could this harm a male audience?

Consider those questions with an open and honest heart. Provide your insights below.

_____
_____
_____
_____

God's true notions are always life-giving and soul-challenging, no matter who is communicating them. Once again, we come up against the only logical explanation for why a woman would be disqualified from preaching and teaching God's true notions— the female human being, simply by being female, carries within her a deficiency that makes her ill-equipped to exercise the gifts of teaching, preaching, and leading.

Think back to when we first began this study and dealt with the premise that women are subordinated because they are deficient when it comes to exercising spiritual authority. Has your viewpoint changed since then? Whether it has or it hasn't, provide your insights below.

_____
_____
_____
_____
_____

Let's review 1 Corinthians 14:22–33 again, though we've briefly touched on it before. Take a moment to read through this portion of Scripture slowly and record anything that pops out at you below.

_____
_____
_____
_____
_____

Verse 23 begins with "so if the *whole church* comes together and everyone speaks in tongues…" and verse 24 follows with "*everyone* is prophesying…" This tells us that even in the Corinthian church, where head coverings were being debated and Paul was having to reign in the flippancy with which some women were behaving, females still exercised verbal ministry gifts in corporate worship to the benefit of everyone (even unbelievers). Lest we become tempted to think that Paul is to be understood as excluding women, verse 26 brings it all into sharp contrast. Record verse 26 below.

_____

_____

_____

_____

_____

_____

_____

_____

This verse makes it clear that, even in the patriarchal Corinthian culture, every brother and sister was expected—indeed directed—to come together, bringing hymns, words of instruction, revelations, tongues, and interpretations. Record verse 31 below as well.

_____

_____

_____

_____

What Paul is calling prophesy here obviously means something different than how we think of prophesy in our day and age. He makes clear that every brother and sister can each bring words of instruction and encouragement to minister to the entire body of believers. The only requisite here is that the person ministering is a believer because we are all members of the royal priesthood—each and every one outfitted for good works that benefit the whole.

How does it make you feel to know that you are a royal priest and that God can use you to bring both instruction and encouragement to anyone—believer or unbeliever, male or female, rich or poor? Take a minute to think this over and respond in the space below.

_____

_____

_____

_____

Though so much more can be said about Spirit-giftedness, this chapter has demonstrated a few key points to help us move forward.

- Humans do not bestow spiritual gifts; only the Holy Spirit of God can do so. Therefore, only the Spirit can determine who each person is meant to instruct, encourage, or edify with their giftings.

- Maleness is not a requirement to receive and/or exercise any of the gifts of the Spirit.

- The Bible doesn't prohibit women from exercising any gift of the Spirit or limit to whom they may minister.

- Spirit-giftedness should be the only requirement for any type of ministry.

- Every believer is now a royal priest because of what Christ accomplished on the cross.

- The only value left to categorizations, such as gender or social status, are in how they help us glorify God in our cultures and communities. Beyond that, hierarchy no longer exists in the Kingdom of God.

- From the beginning, women participated in all forms of ministry, to include verbal ministries of instruction and encouragement.

As we move into our final chapter of this study, I encourage you to take your time with the following discussion questions. Ponder them long and hard before sharing your thoughts with others. Oftentimes, a certain amount of discomfort—and perhaps even pain—comes along with a study this sensitive in nature. We must allow ourselves to feel these things and process them as we go along. Ask the Holy Spirit to open your heart and your eyes and welcome Him in to any discomfort or pain that may come up. Remember that all truth is God's truth, and, therefore, we have nothing to fear through these explorations.

Reflection & Discussion

1. Pastor and author Stuart Briscoe shares this insight he received while studying the parable of the buried talents: "But then like a thunderclap the thought occurred to me: 'What does the Master think of those who bury the gifts of others?' And I knew that I, as a husband, father, and pastor, could do precisely that with the gifts of thousands of women. There and then I asked the Lord, 'Whatever else you can accuse me of, please deliver me from ever being guilty of burying the gifts of those over whom I legitimately exercise some degree of spiritual oversight.'"[12]

2. Consider the number of little girls, teenagers, college age women, young mothers, and grandmothers who have had their talents buried because of a few passages of Scripture that can be effectively counterargued using sound hermeneutical and exegetical principles. Discuss the dangers of burying the talents of girls and women in our church community. What's at stake?

3. Have you ever known a woman—perhaps even yourself—who was obviously gifted in the verbal ministries or gifted in administration but was limited in how she could use her gifts in the body of Christ? Talk about some of your experiences, especially in regard to any reasons you can think of that her good, Spirit-bestowed gifts shouldn't have been used to edify the entire church? Why would God give them those kinds of gifts if not to use them?

4. Consider Deborah (Judges 4–5), Huldah (2 Kings 22:14; 2 Chronicles 34:22), Philip's daughters and, of course, Priscilla's role in the instruction of Apollos (Acts 21:9; 18:26). How can these women's leadership roles be explained if God has created females ill-equipped for such things? Discuss possibilities.

5. Many congregations allow women to teach and instruct young boys but only until a certain age. When does it become unfit for a woman to instruct a young man? Why can she be trusted to instruct boys in their most formative years but not thereafter?

---

[12] Briscoe, Stuart. (2010). Burying Talents. (How I changed my mind about women in leadership: compelling stories from prominent evangelicals) Grand Rapids: Zondervan, 2010.

Patrick and Tessa's Story

They were an old-fashioned couple, Patrick and Tessa. They're friends often ribbed them for being the "Leave it to Beaver" types, and, honestly, they never minded being seen that way. Tessa was the kind of woman who made an art out of homemaking. She thrived in the areas of keeping house, managing schedules, practicing hospitality, and supporting her husband and children in their endeavors. Her finger was always on the pulse of her home, and she was more than content with her role. In fact, she was utterly grateful for it.

Likewise, Patrick was a consummate family man, providing a comfortable life for his family and protecting them in every way. Nothing brought him more satisfaction than sitting around the dinner table at night and listening to his family recount the stories of their days, knowing that the work of his hands made it all possible. Naturally, teachings they'd received throughout the years on gender hierarchy didn't alarm them. Tessa had no desire or call to teach, preach, or lead in any capacity. Patrick fell easily into the role of "leader" in the home, and though he always consulted Tessa with big decisions, they were both comfortable with him making the final call when necessary.

All of this began to change, however, with their daughter, Hannah. She didn't fit any of their pre-conceived notions of "femaleness."

Unlike her older sister, Hannah was always more into athletics than dolls. She'd rather be in the woods than a shopping mall. She was bullied at school for being "like a boy." Instead of being a safe place of refuge, their church wasn't much better. As Hannah got older and didn't conform to the feminine ideal, she was excluded and even ridiculed at times.

Patrick and Tessa were torn. They worried that Hannah wouldn't have a place in church or in a marriage. What kind of life awaited her if she couldn't summon up nurturing femininity? On the other hand, they admired her spunk and strength. They actually enjoyed her unique personality and didn't want her to change to fit in with others' expectations.

As Hannah embarked into womanhood, theological questions they'd never entertained before began to surface.

If Hannah wasn't destined for marriage and motherhood, what was her role in the church?

Their daughter possessed obvious leadership gifts. Why would the Spirit of God give her giftings that their church taught were out-of-bounds for females?

Hannah would never be fit for "women's ministry" in the traditional sense. Yet, she spent hours each week studying the Word of God, and theology lit her world on fire. Where would she find outlets for all that God was doing in her?

For the first time, Patrick and Tessa began to question the difference between tradition and biblical principles. If God's Spirit was now truly being poured out on flesh as they knew the Word of God said, then why was it okay to hold Hannah back from where the Spirit was taking her in the name of traditional female roles? What was the real priority?

That was the question that reverberated between them as they sat up together at night: what was God's real priority for their daughter's life?

Harmony Restored

It could be argued that liberal feminism is wreaking havoc on our society and our homes.

Touting a message that seems to glorify selfish ambition and promulgating outright disdain for males, many in the feminist camp have tainted the waters of the egalitarian message.

It's no wonder, then, that so many in the church are resistant to the idea that God's true notion for His church is that hierarchy has no place. Though the road was a long and rough one, the church finally accepted that social and ethnic hierarchy should be rejected. However, gender hierarchy is not only still practiced, but it is fiercely defended by those who perceive threat to treasured social, familial, and religious norms.

Did Jesus come to destroy cultural norms, or did he come to restore everything that was lost in Eden? If we accept that females are not meant for subordination, and if we reject gender hierarchy in our churches and homes, what will happen to our current constructs? Will chaos ensue?

Oneness

We've come to our final chapter, where we will begin to see God's true notions for His church. We'll start with the urgent and beautiful prayer of King Jesus, spoken right before his betrayal and arrest. Turn to John 17:20–23 and record it below.

_____
_____
_____
_____
_____
_____
_____

For whom is Jesus praying?

_____
_____
_____

Week 9: Harmony Restored

What is His great prayer for all believers?

_____
_____
_____

In verse 22, what does Jesus say He has given all believers?

_____
_____
_____

According to this verse, why are all believers given the glory of God?

_____
_____
_____

What is the purpose of "complete unity," according to verse 23?

_____
_____
_____

If I were to describe the tone of Jesus's prayer here, I would use the word *imploring*. Jesus seems absolutely desperate for those who belong to him to also belong to each other, in complete oneness. The definition of oneness, according to the dictionary, is "the fact or state of being united or whole, though comprised of two or more parts."

Let's think about the concept of something whole that is also comprised of two or more parts, such as the wheel of a bike. The wheel is the whole, and each spoke is a separate entity within the whole, connected by a hub.

This visual helps us understand what Jesus's prayer was all about—wholeness, oneness, and connectedness.

Do you see hierarchy in this image or in the prayer of our Lord? Did Jesus seem concerned that we all know our places in the hierarchy of His church? Consider these questions and record any thoughts you may have below.

_____
_____
_____
_____

Another visual that helps us understand our relationship to Christ and to one another is provided by Jesus in John 15:5–14. Read this portion of Scripture and record verse 5 below.

_____
_____
_____
_____

Here, Jesus likens himself to a vine and his believers to branches. The concept of oneness is found here again as he describes the need for his believers to remain in him and for him to remain in his believers. Jesus goes on to urge his believers to remain in the love of God by keeping his commands. By keeping his commands, our joy will be complete (v. 11). Record verses 12–13 below.

_____
_____
_____
_____

What does verse 13 say is the absolute greatest love anyone can have?

_____
_____
_____

Again, Jesus urges his believers to pursue oneness with him and with one another. He then provides a very practical—yet very difficult—*way to do this, which is by laying down our lives for one another.*

We must pause here and absorb these connections: Jesus offers us oneness with God and full access to His glory and love. If we stay in Him—connected and one—we access this love. Then Jesus says that if we love Him and remain in Him, we will keep his command to love one another with the type of love that requires us to lay down our lives for each other.

What does "lay down your life" imply to you? Provide your thoughts below.

_____
_____
_____
_____
_____
_____

If we are all laying down our lives for one another, where does that leave room for subordinating one another? This is the truth: just like it would be impossible to adopt a philosophy of liberal feminism that coalesced with a philosophy of laying down your life, it is equally impossible to adopt a philosophy of female subordination that does so.

The damaging philosophies of liberal feminism and patriarchy have this in common—they insert hierarchy into human relationships where God never intended it to be.

Edenic Harmony Restored

Let's reflect back on what we learned about God's notions regarding gender harmony as found in the creation account in Genesis.

- Man was created in the image of God, but it was not good for him to be alone. God made woman, also created in the image of God, to be an equal partner in life and in work.

- Man and woman existed together in complete harmony, with no system of hierarchy in place between them. They co-labored to order the world, without shame or suspicion.

- It wasn't until the Fall that shame, suspicion, competition, and hierarchy entered the male/female relationship, all of which are distortions of God's true notions.
- God, in His gracious provision, cast the man and woman out of the garden so that they could not partake of the tree of eternal life and seal themselves in this fallen state for eternity.

Now let's reflect on what we know about Christ's work through his life, death, and resurrection. Christ's entire mission was to redeem and restore that which was lost at the Fall (Galatians 3:13; Hebrews 9:15; 1 Peter 1:18–19; Colossians 1:12–14).

Let's examine Colossians 1:20–22. Record the verses below.

This verse is particularly powerful because it's essentially talking about a complete reversal of the curse that humankind lived under until Christ's work was complete. Circle the phrase "things on earth or things in heaven." What does this tell you about the thoroughness of Christ's reconciliation? Provide your thoughts below.

How did Christ accomplish this powerful, all-encompassing reconciliation, according to verse 20?

_____
_____
_____
_____

Verse 21 takes us back to Eden by reminding us that once we were alienated from God. Along with the first man and woman, we were exiled from intimate fellowship with our Creator. Indeed, we were enemies in our minds because of evil behavior.

What does it mean to be an enemy of God, in your mind? Connect this with the mindset that began creeping in at the Fall.

_____
_____
_____
_____

Verse 22 is very clear: through Christ's death, we are reconciled to God. We are presented to God as holy. Look carefully at the last phrase of verse 22.

Without blemish and free from accusation.

This verse is one of many which proclaim that what was lost in Eden is being restored in Christ. What does this mean for females in the body of Christ?

- We are no longer subject to the emotional, relational, or spiritual bondage of the curse. Jesus is restoring all that has been lost and has reconciled us completely to God.

- We are without blemish and free from accusation, which includes: being more prone to deception; having any inferiority to anyone else; having inherent limitations on spiritual giftedness based upon our gender alone; and having any shame or trauma related to our female humanity.

What does this mean for males in the body of Christ?

- They are no longer subject to the emotional, relational, or spiritual bondage of the curse. Jesus is restoring all that has been lost and has reconciled them completely to God.

- They are now without blemish or accusation, which includes: being prone to aggression and power hunger; having their worth defined by their status or achievements; having to shoulder the brunt of life's burdens alone; and having any shame or trauma related to their male humanity.

What does this mean for both males and females in the body of Christ?

- We are restored to ourselves and to one another.

- Shame, suspicion, manipulation, and power struggles do not define our relationships any longer.

- Sinful systems of hierarchy can be replaced with systems of Spirit-led harmony.

- In Christ, our eternal life has been restored so we can be assured that this beautiful harmony will continue forever. There is no longer any reason for fear.

Let's turn to Romans 15:5–7. Record the verses below.

_____
_____
_____
_____
_____
_____

Paul is charging the church to "accept one another" in order to bring "praise to God." The church was forming faster than anyone could tally. One home church after another was springing up, and it was becoming clear that Christ's body was going to be diverse, comprised of Jews and Gentiles, rich and poor, slave and free, male and female. For God-honoring harmony to reign, it was going to be absolutely imperative that the believers learn to accept one another.

The ESV translates the Greek word *homothymadon* as "harmony," and the NIV translates it as "with one accord." It's literal meaning, according to Strong's Greek Concordance, is "of the same passion." It describes people who share "like precious faith," creating a God-produced unity between them (cf. 2 Pet 1:1–2). Here they "have the same mind" (the Lord's thoughts) because each receives the same revelation of His Word. See this powerful application of (*homothymadón*) in Acts 1:14, 2:1 and 46, 4:24, 5:12, and 8:6.[13]

---

[13] Strong, J. (1995). Enhanced Strong's Lexicon. Woodside Bible Fellowship.

It would be helpful to follow the lead of the Greek reference above and visit those verses mentioned. Let's turn to Acts 1:14 and record it below.

_____
_____
_____
_____

Notice that Acts 1:14 hones in on the fact that "the women" and "Mary the mother of Jesus" are included—not excluded—from the God-produced unity that brings "the Lord's thoughts" because each was receiving the *same* revelation of His Word.

Acts 2 is a powerful example of *homothymadon* and showcases what happens when the body of believers—both male and female—come together in harmony. Read the entire chapter and record your observations below.

_____
_____
_____
_____
_____

Homothymadon

ho·mo·thü·mä·do'n

Hebrew Lexicon: Adverb: With one mind, with one accord, with one pasion

Acts 2 opens up with the harmonious gathering of God's people in Jerusalem— "They were all together in one place." How do we know that there were women gathered alongside the men? When Peter addressed the crowd, he recited the prophesy spoken by the prophet Joel. Record verses 17 and 18 below.

_____

_____

_____

_____

_____

The prophet Joel had a vision of the last days, when God's Spirit would be poured out on all people. This was an inclusive and egalitarian vision—young and old, male and female, every tongue and tribe, every social class would be included under the umbrella of "all people" and "everyone who calls upon the name of the Lord." What do these verses say, specifically, that women will do alongside men?

_____

_____

_____

The word "prophecy" as translated in the NIV in Acts 2:17 comes from the Greek word *prophetes*, which means literally "one who speaks forth by the inspiration of God." This is the actual notation from Strong's Greek Concordance: "A prophet (4396 /*prophḗtēs*) declares the mind (message) of God, which sometimes predicts the future (foretelling) and, more commonly, *speaks forth* His message for a particular situation. 4396 / *prophḗtēs* ("a prophet") then is someone inspired by God to *foretell* or *tell-forth* (*forthtell*) the Word of God."[14]

Acts 2:17–18 can accurately be read this way:

> In the last days, God says, I will pour out my spirit on all people. Your sons and daughters will speak forth by the inspiration of God, forthtelling the Word of God . . . Even on my servants, both men and women, I will pour out my Spirit in those days, and they will speak forth by the inspiration of God, forthtelling the Word of God.

We see here a direct parallel between the harmony of the body of Christ and the power of the Holy Spirit to equip both men and women to forthtell the Word of God. What we do not see here is any implication of hierarchy, inferiority, exclusion, or prohibition of any kind on either males or females, when it comes to speaking forth the Word of God in a public setting for the edification of others and the persuasion of the lost.

---

[14] Strong, J. (1995). Enhanced Strong's Lexicon. Woodside Bible Fellowship.

Consider the implications of males and females working in Spirit-led harmony to forthtell the Word of God. Can you think of any reason why this would be detrimental? Can you think of any reason why this would be beneficial? Provide your insights below.

_____
_____
_____
_____
_____
_____

If a woman is Spirit-led and Spirit-gifted to speak forth God's Word, how could this be harmful to anyone? The obvious answer is that it can't be harmful. Spirit leading and Spirit gifting can only ever be life-giving. Whether the audience hearing the message is male, female, lost or saved, if it is spoken from the Holy Spirit, it is both authoritative and beneficial. What higher authority does any church have than the Spirit of God to deny women expression?

No Respecter of Persons

Let's turn now to Acts 10 and read the entire chapter. Record your observations below.

_____
_____
_____
_____

Peter has seen some things, hasn't he? First, he has his life completely upended and redeemed by the Messiah. Then, he becomes the leader of a movement that begins to sweep the region—complete with signs, wonders, and miracles. Then, he has this vision in which God chastises him for his inability to see the new thing that had begun with Christ.

God's corrections were being made; but Peter was human and, like all of us, he was having a hard time letting go of the old system.

Clean and unclean. Jew and Gentile. Slave and free. Law and grace. Male roles and female roles.

These classifications were all he had ever known. They held his world together in many ways. Things didn't make sense without them. He was struggling to understand how order would be kept and how he would conceptualize the world without these constructs.

Suddenly, jarringly, God was saying, "Do not call anything impure that God has made clean." (v. 15).

With all of the miracles happening before his very eyes, it's no wonder that Peter made the confession that he did in Acts 10:34. Record the verse below.

_____
_____
_____
_____
_____

The KJV translates this vere as ". . . I understand that God is no respecter of persons." The NIV translates it as "God does not show favoritism." The phrase comes from the Greek words prosópon and lambanó which, together, literally means, "an acceptor of a face" or "one who shows partiality."

Prosópon

Ancient Greek; a person's outword appearance

Lambanó

Ancient Greek; To recieve, get, take, or lay hold of.

In other words, God is not impartial to anyone. The obvious connection with the concept of female subordination is that God is not a respecter of maleness. Setting aside tradition and assumption, nowhere in the actual Word of God does it say that our Creator's true notions were that males would be superior to females or that females were inherently inferior. Nowhere in God's Word does it say that males are the only ones gifted with the ability to preach and teach (speaking forth God's Word). Nowhere does it say that males are blessed with leadership abilities or certain qualities for exercising authority that females lack. In fact, the Word of God is replete with examples and teachings of just the opposite of all of that.

At the very bottom of the notion of God-ordained female subordination is the belief that God is, indeed, partial to maleness. The underlying core argument is that males are endowed with a little something extra that enables them to exercise all of the spiritual gifts, to exercise authority over females, and to be the ultimate spiritual leaders in church and at home.

This is the same logic strain that led Peter to elevate Jews over Gentiles. It's the same logic strain that found the Corinthian church instituting a class system at the Lord's table (1 Corinthians 11:17–34). To their everlasting shame, it's also the same logic strain that allowed Christian slave owners in America to keep human beings as property.

It's the same logic strain that continues to produce human systems of hierarchy over God's system of harmony.

Consider that logic strain and juxtapose against what we've read in Acts 10 and elsewhere. Do you see truth in the idea that God respects maleness in the sense that it is a requirement for spiritual giftedness and leadership? Explain below.

_____
_____
_____
_____
_____

Think about why God went to such lengths to get through to Peter that the old system of hierarchy had passed away and was being replaced by a new way. Why do you think this was so important to God?

_____
_____
_____
_____

Acts 10:25–26 shows Cornelius falling down before Peter's feet in reverence, absolutely honored that a man of God would enter his home. The NIV says "Peter made him get up," stating "Stand up . . . I am only a man myself." Peter's vision from heaven, coupled with all that he'd seen and been taught by Christ, combined with the outpouring of the Holy Spirit on a diverse Church, had left him humbled and with a healthy sense of who he really was in the grand scheme of things. He entered the house of a Gentile and led every uncircumcised person there to the Lord.

Later, when Peter was explaining these events and his new worldview to the offended Jews in Jerusalem, he said something very telling. Record Acts 11:17 below.

_____
_____
_____
_____
_____

To what gift is Peter referring?

_____

This is so powerful! Peter is emphasizing that when the Holy Spirit of God comes upon a believer—no matter who he or she is—there is nothing that anyone can do to prevent the outcome.

Who am I to stand in the way? He asks. What was the outworking of the baptism of the Holy Spirit at Cornelius's house? Every one of those uncircumcised people began "speaking in tongues and praising God."

They gained spiritual expression, immediately. Spirit-filled expression is the first thing that happens when a new believer is filled with the Holy Spirit. Again and again in Scripture, we find that the Holy Spirit causes the people of God to speak forth the Word, praise God, speak in tongues, encourage, edify, rebuke, teach, preach, and pray. Therefore, who can stand against the spiritual expression of any believer?

Can you think of any ways in which true spiritual expression, unhindered by a system of hierarchy, could be harmful to the body of Christ? Provide your thoughts below.

_____
_____
_____

In the Corinthian and Ephesian churches, as we discovered in previous chapters, many new believers (both male and female) were speaking forth in ignorance and haste. Therefore, God inspired Paul to provide guidelines for those who would teach the Word of God. The complementarian argument that women should not be allowed to preach or teach in corporate worship begins to lose cohesion when we consider the role of the Holy Spirit in gifting and empowering women.

If the Holy Spirit of God gifts a woman with teaching and preaching ability, she applies herself to rigorous study of God's Word, and she speaks forth a message in the power of the Holy Spirit with a humble, loving heart, what could go wrong? How could a woman like this deliver this solid message to a group of other women, but if she spoke the same message to a mixed audience, it becomes dangerous?

Pause here and give this the reflection it deserves. Our churches are sending a schizophrenic message to their congregations and to the world-at-large.

On the one hand, women are encouraged to learn the truth of God and to live it with their whole hearts. On the other hand, they are discouraged from sharing the fruits of their spiritual lives with the entire body of believers. To make matters worse, they're not being discouraged because of a lack of education, a lack of cultural appropriateness, or a lack of Spirit-giftedness or ability. They're being discouraged—and in many cases forbidden—because of a lack of maleness.

The only thing holding a woman back, if she is gifted for preaching, teaching, and leadership, is her femaleness.

Miraculous Mutuality

At the end of the day, it seems that one of the greatest deterrents to evangelical Christians openly and universally rejecting female subordination is the fear that it would be akin to opening a Pandora's Box of feminism, rebellion, dissension, and throwing off of convention.

What I hope has been made clear throughout this study is that the purpose of rejecting hierarchy is to open ourselves up to beautiful harmony instead. What would it look like if our churches and families adopted a theology of love verses a theology of gender roles?

Let's look at Colossians, chapter 3, which is the perfect picture of what life would look like if lived without hierarchy. Read the entire chapter and record your observations below.

_____
_____
_____
_____
_____
_____
_____
_____

Paul is imploring the Colossian church to put off anything that belongs to the "earthly nature" (v. 5) and, instead, put on the "new self, which is being renewed in knowledge in the image of is Creator" (v. 10). What sort of knowledge is being renewed, according to verse 11?

_____
_____
_____
_____

Here we arrive at the concept of oneness again. Christ is all and is in all. Every believer is in Christ, and He encompasses the entire church. What does one look like who is indwelt by Christ? What is the fabric of this newness of which they are clothed? Verses 12–14 tell us about these virtues.

- Compassion
- Kindness
- Humility
- Gentleness
- Patience
- Bearing with others
- Forgiving

What does verse 14 say must be put on over all of these virtues and why is it important?

_____
_____
_____
_____

Love is the binder, the cohesive force, between these virtues and between all believers of Jesus Christ. Record verses 15–16 below.

_____
_____
_____
_____
_____

God's notion is that Christ's body be at peace and as one. His true desire is that the message of Christ dwell "richly" among His people as they practice spiritual expression. Do you see any evidence that women are excluded from the teaching and admonishing that is supposed to be happening in the united body of Christ? Is there any hierarchy mentioned here or any restrictions? No, there is no hint of either because God's expectation for His people is found in verse 17: "Whatever you do, whether in word or in deed, do it all in the name of the Lord Jesus, giving thanks to God the Father through him." When a harmonious body of believers is doing everything in the name of Christ and is empowered by the Holy Spirit of God, there is no need for hierarchy.

Even as Colossians 3 concludes with Paul's direct handling of culturally hierarchical relationships, God's true notions—those corrections that are beginning to be made—shine through. Culturally, wives were expected to submit to their husbands. Paul addresses this head on and affirms that Christian wives should continue to do so. Directly after this, he provides counterbalance in instructing husbands to love their wives and refrain from being harsh with them (vv. 18–19). Children are instructed to obey their parents, and, as a counterbalance, fathers are told to refrain from embittering their children (vv. 20–21). Slaves are entreated to obey their masters in everything and at all times, while masters are tasked with being fair and humble (vv. 22, 25).

The body of Christ was rising up and taking its place in a broken system. God's true notions were working their way into the broken system, taking on one distortion at a time. The Western church has progressed to a point where it is a given that husbands are not to be harsh with their wives, where fathers are expected to go beyond simply using restraint with their children and they are to actually love them. We've rejected slavery completely and have worked to overturn this evil wherever it is found. In short, the corrections of God are continuing to work their way in, challenging believers to open their hearts and eyes up to the timeless heart of God, requiring a rejection of old ways in favor of the embracing of God's true notions.

Ephesians 5:21 through 6:9 continues this theme and, indeed, expands upon it. The concept of mutuality comes alive as Paul begins with verse 21. Record it below.

_____
_____
_____
_____
_____
_____
_____
_____

Here, Paul is admonishing all believers to submit to one another. Then, he goes on to describe culturally hierarchical relationships again and expands upon what mutuality will look like in the cultural context of his day. Wives, again, are told to submit to their husbands as they do the Lord, in everything. The startling part comes in verse 25, when Paul gives instruction to husbands on how they are to love their wives. Record this verse below.

_____
_____
_____

Wives are to submit to their husbands and husbands are to give themselves up for their wives. Verse 33 sums this mysterious mutuality up. Record this verse below.

_____
_____

Again, Paul is emphasizing a mutual relationship in which the husband loves his wife as he loves himself and the wife is to respect her husband. In a relationship where one partner is seeking to give up her own will for the sake of the other and the other partner is doing the same, where does subordination come into play? Once again, we arrive at the conclusion that it is not possible to insert hierarchy in a relationship such as this. Both partners are too busy putting themselves last and seeking harmony to subordinate the other.

What happens when there is a decision that must be made and disagreement exists between husband and wife? The answer to that question lies in all that we've learned about what it means to have Christ alive in our hearts and the Holy Spirit working harmony in our souls—both partners stay at the drawing board until a mutually satisfying decision is made.

It's that simple. There's no need to fear what will happen to marriages if both partners are empowered to make decisions and exercise spiritual agency, as long as they are committed to harmony and oneness in Christ.

> The beauty of God's perfect design is that in both partners' willingness to lose their lives, they find their lives. Everyone wins!

Think about this: Many married couples who consider themselves complementarian actually operate in an egalitarian manner, for all practical purposes. Usually, in healthy Christian marriages, wives make their opinions known and husbands take those opinions into consideration and often make decisions that please both parties. Why do you think this is the case? Provide your thoughts below.

_____
_____
_____
_____
_____
_____

Galatians 5:13–14 gives us another picture of what mutuality will look like in the church. Record these verses below.

_____
_____
_____
_____

Believers are called to be free! Make note of Paul's inclusive language—"You, my brothers and sisters . . ." in verse 13. Males and females are called to be completely and totally free. However, we are not to use our freedom to indulge our flesh. Circle the phrase in verse 13 that describes how we are to use our freedom.

We are meant to use our glorious freedom to serve one another humbly in love. Where does subordination fit in with this picture? Again, it doesn't. It can't. When we are all serving one another in humble love, we have no time or any reason to subordinate each other.

Let's look at Philippians 2:1–8. Take a moment to read this passage and record your observations below.

___

___

___

___

___

___

___

One in spirit. One in mind. Humbly valuing others over ourselves. Having the mindset of Christ in our relationships with each other – making ourselves nothing by taking the very nature of a servant.

This is what miraculous mutuality looks like. Each believer valuing what the Holy Spirit has deposited inside of the other, *even more than the value he gives himself*. Each believer *making nothing of herself* and, instead, serving those around her.

In this beautiful snapshot of God's intentions for His people, where is there room for usurping of authority or silencing of expression? Where is the need to subordinate or dominate? Yes, we're belaboring a point, but it's necessary to do so.

The stakes are high. Half of God's church is being benched while the harvest is ripe in the field (John 4:27–42)! Women who carry within themselves the Holy Spirit of God Almighty and the powerful giftings of heaven are being pushed away from the table and told to bury their talents, while the souls who need what they have are perishing.

Men who desire intimacy, partnership, and rest from the hardships of life are suffering silently while shouldering the weight of authority in their churches, marriages, and families. According to Scripture, this is not only needless but contrary to God's desires.

Could it be that it's not so much theological differences but a *fear of losing control* that is holding the church back from the glorious possibilities mutuality will bring?

After all, empowered wives will only empower their husbands. Empowered mothers will only enrich their children. Empowered women will only edify, encourage, and share godly wisdom with their congregations.

Empowered women operating in mutuality with empowered men have always been, and will always be, a force to be reckoned with in the spiritual realm.

Satan knew this when he slithered between them in the Garden of Eden, and Satan knows it now as he continues to sew seeds of suspicion, shame, and power hunger between them to this day.

Each place where we see God's vision for His church, we're presented with harmony, mutuality, oneness, and acceptance. Remember, these are God's notions of what is good for us, and so we can trust that our churches, our marriages, our families, and our world will only be made better by living out these beautiful ideas and seeing these corrections through until that glorious day when His will is finally completely done "on earth as it is in heaven" (Matthew 6:10).

Reflection & Discussion

1. Throughout the course of this study, you've been asked to stretch your thinking in many areas, but perhaps none is more challenging than the consideration that a fear of losing control is at least part of what is fueling the defense of female subordination in the church. Reflect on and discuss what role you think fear could play in this issue, on either side of the argument.

   _____
   _____
   _____
   _____
   _____
   _____
   _____
   _____

2. God said to Peter, "Do not call unclean what I have called clean," even as Peter struggled to make sense of the end of a system that had always given order to his world. Reflect on and discuss the parallels between Peter's situation and the one the church is faced with today, as the gender debate continues to wear on.

   _____
   _____
   _____
   _____
   _____
   _____
   _____
   _____

3. King Jesus washed the feet of his disciples, much to their discomfort and shock. He remarked afterward, "Now that I, your Lord and Teacher, have washed your feet, you also should wash one another's feet. I have set and example that you should do as I have done for you" (John 13:14–15). How can "feet-washing servants" subordinate one another? Is it possible? Reflect on this and discuss the implications for female subordination in the church.

___

4. Harmony is always God's true notion for what is good, over and above human systems of hierarchy. Why is harmony preferable to hierarchy? Is it possible for a system of spiritual hierarchy to showcase God's radical servant-love to the world?

___

Final Thoughts from the Author

The writing of this Bible study was a labor of love that came about due to the gentle, but constant, insistence of many of my sisters and brothers in Christ. Our current cultural climate is one in which the church is facing hard questions, not only from within her ranks, but from the secular world-at-large. We're all grappling with the concepts of hierarchy, female subordination, and God's true notions about women. I approached this study with a humble resolve to face the hard questions head-on and to do so with fairness and integrity.

It's my prayer that I achieved this goal because the world is watching us and bringing honor to God is all that matters.

What kept me going, through frustrations and setbacks, were the faces and voices of so many confused and hurting Christians whom I've met throughout the years. Women—guilty, lonely, lacking purpose, and spiritual renewal. Men—overwhelmed, disconnected, and dissatisfied. I kept their stories at the forefront of my mind and of my prayers as I scoured the Bible, commentaries, and lexicons. I lack a seminary education, but my passion for God's true notions about gender harmony forced me to do the work of a theologian anyway.

What I found in my studies is that God's timeless heart for His people is made obvious in His Word, even when apparent contradictions are present, the perfect meanings of words are elusive and sociocultural circumstances are murky. God left us the beauty of His Word, written and kept safe by many human hands throughout thousands of years, so that we'd know His love, our worth, and the purpose of the human saga. I continue to believe that, as the Church progresses toward that day when she is finally completely united with Christ, she will continue to adjust to God's new order—His Kingdom come—until every person has an equally humble, and yet honored, seat at the table of her Lord.

To the brothers who have read this study, I pray that you found hope for a powerful intimacy with your sisters, mothers, daughters, and wives, which has too-often been denied you since the ancient garden. The world needs your particular reflection of the image of God, with all of its beauty, strength, and vulnerability. You've had to shoulder heavy burdens—so many times without the spiritual and emotional aid of your perfectly fitted female counterparts. I pray you find rest and that we, as your sisters, can help you with some of the load.

To the sisters who have read this study, I pray that you step into your Spirit-filled empowerment with urgency. We are in desperate need, in these dark times, of your particular reflection of the image of God, with all of its beauty, strength, and vulnerability. The world is crying out for the spiritual expression that is bursting at the seams of your hearts and your lips. I pray that this study helps you be brave enough to cast off: learned helplessness, the silencing of yourselves, and the cult of nurturance that so often comes at the expense of the hearing and obeying of God's Word (Luke 11:27–28).

Recognize that you have already been seated at the table of our Lord.

No one can take your seat, ask you to leave or silence your voice. Your seat is secured for all time by nothing less than the precious blood of Christ. Go, daughters of God, and speak forth that Good News which saved you.

Notes

Unless otherwise noted, Scripture quotations are taken from the Holy Bible, New International Version®, NIV®. Copyright© 1973, 1978, 1984, 2011 by Biblica, Inc.™ Used by permission of Zondervan. All rights reserved worldwide. www.zondervan.com. The "NIV" and "New International Version:" are trademarks registered in the United States Paten and Trademark Office by Biblica, Inc.™

---

1. Strong, J. (1995). Enhanced Strong's Lexicon. Woodside Bible Fellowship.

2. Strong, J. (1995). Enhanced Strong's Lexicon. Woodside Bible Fellowship.

3. Strong, J. (1995). Enhanced Strong's Lexicon. Woodside Bible Fellowship.

4. Foh, Susan, "What is a Woman's Desire?" WTJ 37 (1975): 376-83.

5. Latin Vulgate, Holy Bible Online.

6. Utley, R. J. Paul's Letters to a Troubled Church: I and II Corinthians (Vol 6) (Marshall, TX: Bible Lessons International, 2002).

7. Swanson, J. Dictionary of Biblical Languages with Semantic Domains: Greek (New Testament) (electronic ed.) (Oak Harbor: Logos Research Systems, Inc., 1997).

8. Giles, Kevin. The Trinity and Subordinationism: The Doctrine of God and the Contemporary Gender Debate (Downers Grove, Ill: Intervarsity Press, 2002).

9. Fee, Gordon. First Epistle to the Corinthians, Revised Edition (Eerdmans, 2014), 571.

10. Fee, Gordon. Praying and Prophesying in the Assemblies: 1 Corinthians 11:2-16. (Discovering Biblical Equality: Complementarity without Hierarchy). Downers Grove, IL, Intervarsity Press, 2005.

11. Fee, Gordon. 2005). Male and Female in the New Creation. Discovering Biblical Equality: Complementarity without Hierarchy. Intervarsity Press: Downers Grove, IL.

12. Briscoe, Stuart. (2010). Burying Talents. (How I changed my mind about women in leadership: compelling stories from prominent evangelicals) Grand Rapids: Zondervan, 2010.

13 Strong, J. (1995). Enhanced Strong's Lexicon. Woodside Bible Fellowship.

14 Strong, J. (1995). Enhanced Strong's Lexicon. Woodside Bible Fellowship.

About the Author

Amber H. Jones is a professional writer, speaker and shameless gold digger. Her mission is to find God's gold in every story. She holds a B.S. in Psychology and a M.S. in Human Services Counseling, which she uses every day in the golden chaos of her household.

You can find her at www.amberhjones.com where she blogs about the gold she finds in the life she's built with her husband of twenty years and their seven children. Her inspiring weekly podcast, "Gold Digger: God's Gold in Every Story" can be found on iTunes.

More From the Author

WWW.AMBERHJONES.COM

Made in the USA
San Bernardino, CA
19 October 2018